PROTECTING THE
TO READ

A How-To-Do-It Manual for
School and Public Librarians

ANN K. SYMONS
CHARLES HARMON

ILLUSTRATIONS BY PAT RACE

HOW-TO-DO-IT MANUALS
FOR LIBRARIANS

NUMBER 60

NEAL-SCHUMAN PUBLISHERS, INC.
New York, London

Published by Neal-Schuman Publishers, Inc.
100 Varick Street
New York, NY 10013

Printed and bound in the United States of America.

Library of Congress Cataloging-in-Publication Data

Symons, Ann.
   Protecting the right to read : a how-to-do-it manual for school and public
librarians / by Ann K. Symons and Charles Harmon ; illustrations by Pat
Race.
     p. cm. — (A how-to-it manual for school and public
librarians ; 60)
   Includes bibliographical references (p.   ) and index.
   ISBN 1-55570-216-3 (alk. paper)
   1. Public libraries—Censorship—United States. 2. School libraries—
Censorship—United States. I. Harmon, Charles. II. Title. III. Series:
How-to-do-it manuals for school and public librarians ; no. 60.
Z711.4.S95   1995
025.2'13'0973—dc20   95-42444

DEDICATION

To John and Joel for their love and support. . . . A.K.S.

To Gerald and Pepper . . . the anchors of my life. C.H.

To our professional colleagues whose dedication to and
knowledge of intellectual freedom serve as an inspiration to us
and thousands of other librarians.

ACKNOWLEDGMENTS

The authors wish to express their heartfelt thanks and appreciation to the following individuals and organizations without whose support, patience, and generosity this book would have never been possible.

Judith F. Krug and the American Library Association's Office for Intellectual Freedom for their generous permission to reprint essential documents. Judy's advice, support, and encouragement in support of intellectual freedom are unwavering and invaluable.

Patricia Glass Schuman, president of Neal-Schuman Publishers, Inc., who has encouraged and mentored these two first-time book authors as well as countless others who have contributed to the library literature.

June Pinnell-Stephens, president of the Freedom to Read Foundation, ALA Intellectual Freedom Committee member, and Fairbanks Public Library staff member who was kind enough to read this manuscript and whose wise suggestions improved it immeasurably.

The Juneau (Alaska) School District, the *Juneau Empire*, the Cuyahoga County Public Library, the Minnessota Coalition Against Censorship, the National Council of Teachers of English, and the National Education Association for their permission to reprint documents.

CONTENTS

FIGURES

INTRODUCTION

Intellectual freedom forms the very foundation for library service, just as brick and mortar form the foundations of our library buildings and silicon chips and fiber optic cable undergird the virtual library's infrastructure. Just as democracy would be a farce without the First Amendment, without the liberty to debate and criticize the government that freedom of speech gives us, libraries would be merely sanitized warehouses full of harmless, impotent information without intellectual freedom, the basic premise that writers have a right to be read and people have a right to read, hear, and view whatever they want.

The intended audience for *Protecting the Right to Read: A How-to-Do-It Manual for School and Public Librarians* is the public librarian or school library media specialist who needs to develop new policies or update existing policies. Librarians in such situations often are faced both with reinventing the wheel (i.e., writing coherent, sound policies with little help) and with explaining to administrators, teachers, users, and/or board members what intellectual freedom is and why it is important.

The arrangement of this book is intended to help such librarians:

- Chapter 1, "Intellectual Freedom Principles," opens with a scenario set in a library in which intellectual freedom does not exist. The chapter goes on to explain the unique role libraries play in meeting the First Amendment's guarantee of free speech. It introduces the Library Bill of Rights, its interpretations, the ALA Code of Ethics, and the essential nature of user confidentiality. The chapter looks at individual clauses in both the Code of Ethics and the Library Bill of Rights and explains their applicability to common library situations so as to emphasize the everyday relevance of intellectual freedom to library operations.
- Chapter 2, "Library Policies and Intellectual Freedom," moves from the fundamental principle of intellectual freedom to its implementation in individual libraries. Such implementation necessarily begins with the review and adoption of policies that guide the library's day-to-day operations. The selection policy and appropriate criteria for selection are emphasized. The crucial importance of having policies adopted by governing authorities and making sure that policies aren't just filed away is stressed.

- Chapters 3 and 4, "Considerations Specific to Public Libraries" and "Considerations Specific to School Libraries," explore intellectual freedom situations specific to these two types of libraries. They both move from the more general principles and policies discussed in the first two chapters to the specific administrative and service environments of school and public libraries. For example, chapter 3 discusses such public library concerns as meeting room rules and regulations, the charging of fees, and youth access to adult materials. Chapter 4 discusses the school library within the broader context of today's educational scene, why school libraries must uphold intellectual freedom if they are to carry out *Information Power*'s vision, and how school library media specialists can work with teachers and parents.

- Chapter 5, "Protecting Intellectual Freedom on the Information Superhighway," discusses the brave new world of the Internet and the intellectual freedom challenges it brings to public and school libraries. The chapter looks at the Internet as one of many resources available in the library and applies traditional intellectual freedom tenets to an increasingly popular technology. The chapter both recommends solutions particular libraries have devised for dealing with these complex challenges and refers readers to resources on the Internet for further information and examples.

- Chapters 6 and 7, "The Reconsideration Process" and "A Reconsideration Case Study: *Daddy's Roommate*," are companion chapters. The first defines reconsideration in its various incarnations, ranging from informal reconsideration to a formal request for reconsideration filed with the library director. Reconsideration policies and procedures are discussed, specific examples are presented, the role of the reconsideration committee is examined, and specific tips for dealing with a public hearing are given. The case study chapter deals with today's most frequently challenged title. It explores a challenge filed in four schools in one district and looks at how challenges are as often symbolic of a clash in values as they are disagreements with a particular title.

- Chapter 8, "The Librarian and the Censorship Challenge," builds on everything that has come before. It presents practical tips for surviving a formal challenge based on philosophy, approved policy, and a support network. The chapter emphasizes understanding the tactics that organized censorship groups use and being prepared for them.

- Chapter 9, "Trends and Issues in Intellectual Freedom," looks at censorship yesterday and today as well as makes predictions about four areas that will affect the freedom to read tomorrow. These four issues are: youth access to library resources, the place of religious materials in library collections, gay and lesbian materials, and multiculturalism.
- Chapter 10, the book's conclusion, briefly brings together the various areas discussed in the preceding chapters and looks at two recent incidents in an attempt to bring the challenges and opportunities intellectual freedom presents to life.
- Appendixes A, B, and C present the full text of documents too lengthy to include in the text. These include interpretations of the Library Bill of Rights, documents related to the case study, and sample policies from various organizations.
- The bibliography points readers to sources of further information.

As the book covers philosophy, policy, and practice, it necessarily ranges from discussing abstract concepts to practical "how-to-do-it" tips. The authors hope this approach will facilitate both explaining why intellectual freedom is essential and demonstrating how to ensure its survival in your library.

In covering the "why it needs to be done," we have tried both to present the overwhelming importance of intellectual freedom to all aspects of library service and to demonstrate how ALA's Library Bill of Rights and its interpretations can and should be the starting point for the development of almost all library policies. In approaching the "how to do it," we cast a wide net for existing policies and procedures, talked with librarians across the country about their policies, and detailed a step-by-step approach for moving from an abstract notion of intellectual freedom to a concrete implementation of protection for the rights of all users to read, view, and hear information and ideas in a supportive environment.

Rather than treating intellectual freedom as a defensive maneuver to be carefully deployed in case the censor attacks, the book approaches the topic as one of the fundamental tenets of the profession—as one of the reasons we chose to be librarians. Preparing selection policies, examining reviews of materials, and upholding the rights of all patrons to use all library resources shouldn't be done because "ALA says you have to do it" or because "I need to document why I bought that book in case someone challenges it," but because that's how good library service is implemented.

As well as approaching the topic from this philosophical foundation, the authors recognize and deal with the current political and social landscape. The chapter on reconsideration, the *Daddy's Roommate* case study, and the chapter on being a librarian during a censorship challenge deal with the realities of a challenge in a forthright manner.

Censorship is on the rise not because as a profession we have gotten sloppy in how we write our selection policies or document individual selection decisions, but because our country's political and social pendulum has been swinging towards the right for several years. As part of a somewhat nostalgic sentiment to return to more "innocent" times, conservative groups seeking to "protect" children have launched well-planned, heavily financed attacks on our country's school boards, school curriculum, arts, and library shelves.

In 1995, Focus on the Family launched an unprecedented attack on ALA's Banned Books Week program which sought to persuade the American public that "book banning" was a fictitious concept in modern society. In fact, statistics cited in this book show that all too many challenges are successful and result in materials being removed from libraries and schools. A new group calling itself "Family Friendly Libraries" was formed with support from conservative organizations. This group seeks to remove the Library Bill of Rights from most libraries' policy manuals and instigate restricted access for youth to library collections. These concerted efforts to change the ways libraries operate will succeed unless America's librarians are both prepared for and are willing to stand up for intellectual freedom.

If this book is successful in helping even one librarian prepare for and defend the right to read, we will have accomplished our objective.

Ann K. Symons
Charles Harmon

1 INTELLECTUAL FREEDOM PRINCIPLES

This chapter looks at the unique role libraries play in helping to ensure the First Amendment's guarantee of freedom of speech. The chapter discusses: the profession's historical commitment to intellectual freedom, its fundamental tenets (the Library Bill of Rights and the ALA Code of Ethics), and the importance of user confidentiality. Integrating these basic principles into everyday library operations is an essential component of a climate in which intellectual freedom can flourish.

WHAT IS INTELLECTUAL FREEDOM AND WHY IS IT IMPORTANT?

Imagine that you're a sixth-grade girl just beginning your first menstrual cycle. You've had a nice talk with your mother about what this means. She suggested that you bring some books home that you'll read together to learn more about the changes your body is going through. You visit your school library, but can't find any sex education books. You ask the librarian. She's very nice about it, but she explains that the school district believes that parents should teach their children about sex without interference from the school. After school, you go to the public library, but there are no sex education books in either the children's or young adult collections. The young adult librarian explains that these collections don't have any sex books because she doesn't believe in giving kids ideas about having sex before marriage. She also tells you that you can't go into the adult collection because access to those books is limited to people over 16 or those accompanied by their parents.

If it's hard to imagine this scenario, it's because the premise that libraries should contain all kinds of information and ideas is fundamental to the evolution of the American library. This concept of intellectual freedom in libraries—the right to receive information—is an essential corollary to the First Amendment's guarantee of free speech. After all, an author's right to write anything he or she wants to is meaningless if people don't have the freedom to read it.

Indeed, libraries have been called the "arsenal of democracy" because of their crucial role in upholding the First Amendment.

President Eisenhower, in a letter delivered to the American Library Association's 1953 Annual Conference, wrote, "The libraries of America are and must ever remain the home of free, inquiring minds. To them, our citizens—of all ages and races, of all creeds and political persuasions—must be able to turn with clear confidence that there they can freely seek the whole truth, unwarped by fashion and uncompromised by expediency."

Libraries are forums for the free exchange of ideas and information. They provide a free people with the information they need to make informed choices. Libraries represent all points of view and, remarkably so for a publically funded institution, are politically neutral. Most Americans understand that libraries contain material covering the full spectrum of information and ideas. They expect that when they visit a library to learn more about a subject, they will find the information they seek. Increasingly, however, some people feel obligated to impose their perception of what is right or good on the broader public arena. In the above scenario, the school library was restrained by a school district that didn't believe in providing information about sex; likewise, the young adult librarian in the public library transferred her own beliefs to her collection development decisions, and library policy restricted minors' access to a large portion of the collection.

Both the school and the public librarians infringed upon this sixth-grade child's (and her mother's) right to know. That this scenario is alien to our conception of what a library does is due, in large part, to our profession's grounding in intellectual freedom principles, which are, in fact, based on the First Amendment to the Constitution, which reads:

> Congress shall make no law respecting an establishment of religion, or prohibiting the free exercise thereof; or abridging the freedom of speech, or of the press; or the right of the people peaceably to assemble, and to petition the Government for a redress of grievances.

The idea that each and every citizen, regardless of status, education, or economic condition is entitled to free access to information is central to the library's mission. This entitlement is a direct extension (or, in legalese, a penumbral right) of the First Amendment's guarantee of free speech because it means nothing that someone can write a revolutionary treatise if such a work cannot be freely found and openly accessible in libraries. It would be the same as if the writer were shouting in a soundproof room.

According to the American Library Association's *Intellectual Freedom Manual*, intellectual freedom "requires the fulfillment of two essential conditions: first, that all individuals have the right to hold any belief on any subject and to convey ideas in any form the individual deems appropriate; second, that society makes an equal commitment to the right of unrestricted access to information and ideas . . . " (American Library Association 1992, ix).

The commitment of librarians to intellectual freedom is important because they exercise a great deal of control over access to information. Since only billionaires can afford to buy anything or everything they want to read, most people are dependent on libraries and librarians to make information and ideas accessible to them. Because of the economics of publishing, librarians exercise a great deal of influence over what publishers print. This economic control over content is similar to that which textbook selectors in Texas and California have over textbook publishers; if Texas and California demand a change in content, the same change is very likely to show up in textbooks across the nation.

Merely professing acceptance of intellectual freedom is easy; applying its principles in controversial situations or situations where professional responsibilities conflict with personal beliefs is hard. Consider a few situations that are likely to occur during the course of a librarian's career:

- A principal tells a school librarian to throw away the swimsuit issue of *Sports Illustrated* because it's "trash that doesn't belong in a decent school."
- The president of a public library's board of trustees gives $10,000 to the library to start a collection of audio CDs but privately tells the library director that he "doesn't want to see any of that obscene rap music" in the collection.
- The local police ask a library director for the name of a borrower whose library book is found in a stolen car.

All three of these situations involve intellectual freedom, and all three require courage on the part of the librarian who seeks to uphold its principles with a very rational—but very firm—"No."

THE PROFESSION'S FUNDAMENTAL TENETS

The institutional internalization of the concept of intellectual freedom makes the American library a unique organization—no other type of agency exists within such a philosophical framework. It's not surprising, then, that intellectual freedom is the unifying theme within our profession's most basic tenets: the American Library Association Code of Ethics and the Library Bill of Rights. The following discussion begins with ethics, since most professions have ethical codes; it then proceeds to the Library Bill of Rights, a document unique to librarianship.

ALA CODE OF ETHICS

Being "professional," according to *Merriam-Webster's Collegiate Dictionary*, is "characterized by or conforming to technical or ethical standards of a profession." The American Library Association's Code of Ethics, reprinted in figure 1-1, comprises the ethical standard for our profession.

How does this code relate to intellectual freedom in everyday situations common to libraries? The first tenet of this code requires that librarians provide the highest level of service to *all* requests for assistance. If a librarian responds pleasantly and fully to a request for help from a patron seeking information on where to vote and then treats as frivolous a patron's request for information on how to pierce his or her nose, the response to the second request was unethical. The second tenet requires librarians to say no to the principal who wants to trash the *Sports Illustrated* swimsuit issue and to have a pleasant but firm chat with the board president who wants to exclude rap music from that wonderful CD collection. (Yes, even if it means losing the $10,000. This is one of those situations where there is no easy way out; it may sound facile and simplistic, but allowing personal interests and tastes to dictate collection policies is antithetical to intellectual freedom.) The third tenet of the code means that librarians can't tell the police who checked out the book found in the stolen car unless the police have a court order requiring the library to do so. The fourth tenet requires librarians to uphold copyright laws and resist efforts to save money by pirating software and exceeding fair use guidelines. Tenets five, six, and eight deal more with library operations than intellectual freedom principles. Tenet seven, however, has definite intellectual freedom implications

FIGURE 1–1 ALA Code of Ethics

As members of the American Library Association, we recognize the importance of codifying and making known to the profession and to the general public the ethical principles that guide the work of librarians, other professionals providing information services, library trustees and library staffs.

Ethical dilemmas occur when values are in conflict. The American Library Association Code of Ethics states the values to which we are committed, and embodies the ethical responsibilities of the profession in this changing information environment.

We significantly influence or control the selection, organization, preservation, and dissemination of information. In a political system grounded in an informed citizenry, we are members of a profession explicitly committed to intellectual freedom and the freedom of access to information. We have a special obligation to ensure the free flow of information and ideas to present and future generations.

The principles in this Code are expressed in broad statements to guide ethical decision making. These statements provide a framework; they cannot and do not dictate conduct to cover particular situations.

I.   We provide the highest level of service to all library users through appropriate and usefully organized resources; equitable service policies; equitable access; and accurate, unbiased, and courteous responses to all requests.

II.   We uphold the principles of intellectual freedom and resist all efforts to censor library resources.

III.   We protect each user's right to privacy and confidentiality with respect to information sought or received and resources consulted, borrowed, acquired or transmitted.

IV.   We recognize and respect intellectual property rights.

V.   We treat co-workers and other colleagues with respect, fairness and good faith, and advocate conditions of employment that safeguard the rights and welfare of all employees of our institutions.

VI.   We do not advance private interests at the expense of library users, colleagues, or our employing institutions.

VII.   We distinguish between our personal convictions and professional duties and do not allow our personal beliefs to interfere with fair representation of the aims of our institutions or the provision of access to their information resources.

VIII.   We strive for excellence in the profession by maintaining and enhancing our own knowledge and skills, by encouraging the professional development of co-workers, and by fostering the aspirations of potential members of the profession.

Adopted June 1995
Reprinted by permission of the American Library Association

and would regard as unethical the young adult librarian's response to the sixth-grade girl's search for sex information presented previously.

Rather than viewing the Code of Ethics as restricting and as something to make our jobs harder, librarians and library staff can use the code as a framework for both making and communicating hard decisions to our colleagues, our supervisors, and our community. By reading the code and making sure that library policies and operating procedures reflect its principles, each librarian can make intellectual freedom as unifying a theme in his or her own library as it is in the profession as a whole.

THE LIBRARY BILL OF RIGHTS

The Library Bill of Rights is ALA's most basic intellectual freedom policy. First adopted by ALA in 1939, it derives from the Des Moines Public Library's "Bill of Rights." It has since been amended by ALA several times. The Library Bill of Rights is reproduced in figure 1-2.

The Library Bill of Rights' six tenets provide philosophical bases for all library policy-making. These basic premises undergird every facet of library operations, from making sure that the collection is accessible to physically challenged users to formulating policies and procedures governing meeting room policies. Understanding these six articles and applying them consistently in day-to-day library operations is the key to ensuring that users are guaranteed the freedoms of a democracy. Librarians do this by incorporating the Library Bill of Rights and its interpretations (longer statements adopted by ALA that explain how the Library Bill of Rights applies to specific situations like access to videotapes) into policy, developing procedures that uphold those policies, and educating board members, staff, and patrons about those policies through good public relations programs.

Implementing the ALA Code of Ethics:

- Understand the statement yourself. If you have questions about it, call your state library association or ALA's Office for Intellectual Freedom (800-545-2433).
- Share it with your staff, your supervisor, your advisory committee, your board, etc., *before* any specific situation arises. Then when a difficult situation arises, you can say, "remember when we talked about ethics. This is a situation where we need to act ethically."
- Be consistent. If you use the code only when you want to, you'll lose both your credibility and the battle when you try to apply it as an argument against someone else's wishes or beliefs.

FIGURE 1–2   Library Bill of Rights

The American Library Association affirms that all libraries are forums for information and ideas, and that the following basic policies should guide their services.

1) Books and other library resources should be provided for the interest, information, and enlightenment of all people of the community the library serves. Materials should not be excluded because of the origin, background, or views of those contributing to their creation.

2) Libraries should provide materials and information presenting all points of view on current and historical issues. Materials should not be proscribed or removed because of partisan or doctrinal disapproval.

3) Libraries should challenge censorship in the fulfillment of their responsibility to provide information and enlightenment.

4) Libraries should cooperate with all persons and groups concerned with resisting abridgment of free expression and free access to ideas.

5) A person's right to use a library should not be denied or abridged because of origin, age, background, or views.

6) Libraries which make exhibit spaces and meeting rooms available to the public they serve should make such facilities available on an equitable basis, regardless of the beliefs or affiliations of individuals or groups requesting their use.

Adopted June 18, 1948; amended February 2, 1961, June 27, 1967, and January 23, 1980, by the ALA Council.

Reprinted by permission of the American Library Association

Article 1

Books and other library resources should be provided for the interest, information, and enlightenment of all people of the community the library serves. Materials should not be excluded because of the origin, background, or views of those contributing to their creation.

The key words here are *all people* and *excluded*.

Libraries serve all people—the whole width and breadth of the community—not just the majority of the population. Just as civil rights laws serve to help realize the fundamental American principle that all people are created equal, the first sentence of this first article of the Library Bill of Rights states explicitly that the library "should" provide resources for "all people" it serves. This means that we have a two-fold obligation: first, to proactively determine whom we serve, and what their interests, needs for information, and needs for enlightenment are; and, second, to provide books and other resources that meet those interests and needs even if we—or those to whom we report— disapprove of or disagree with the materials. Community or demographic surveys done as part of the public library planning process can provide useful information in helping public libraries meet this obligation. Likewise, school libraries can be guided by demographic information commonly available in district offices on the income levels, family structure and religious and cultural backgrounds of students in the school's community. This article also mandates inclusivity and diversity. For example, libraries should provide holiday books that have relevance to all members of the community, books that portray all kinds of family structures, and fiction that appeals to all segments of the community served. Serving "all people of the community" may offend some segment of the community. Protecting the right to read requires us to educate our community about that right *before* a challenge arises. Explaining how upholding one person's rights protects all our rights is often a helpful tactic for this educational process.

The second critical phrase of this article is "should not be excluded." The Library Bill of Rights doesn't dictate that libraries *have* to buy anything; it does prohibit libraries from *excluding* works. This article means that liberals can't exclude Rush Limbaugh and conservatives can't exclude Allen Ginsberg; it means that librarians can't decide not to buy any books by communist authors, Ku Klux Klan members, gay activists, or fundamentalist Christians. Protecting the right to read means extending this article to all selection decisions. Librarian A may not want to buy five copies of the latest hate-mongering, fear-inspring, xenophobic commentary or Librarian B may not want to buy the new autobiography by a pro-choice activist, but both must bend over backwards to ensure that they aren't consciously or unconsciously excluding titles they personally find distasteful or offensive.

Article 2

Libraries should provide materials and information presenting all points of view on current and historical issues. Materials should not be proscribed or removed because of partisan or doctrinal disapproval.

This article, like the first, is simple: the key words are *all points of view* and *should not be proscribed*. In practice, the two sentences are frequently related.

Libraries have an obligation to provide materials representing all points of view, both popular and unpopular. This means the collection needs to encompass all sides of debates involving such touchy issues as abortion, gay rights, and health care reform. We must do this if libraries are to be "forums for information and ideas" as described in the preamble to the Library Bill of Rights. Otherwise, we run the risk of becoming associated with a particular viewpoint and lose our credibility as a resource for informed decision making. This article is as important in school libraries as it is in public libraries. If we want students to learn to research issues to make intelligent decisions, we must provide them with access to information on the "politically correct" side of the issue as well as to what some might label the "dubious" side of the issue, and all viewpoints in the intervening spectrum.

Adhering to this article can be difficult in practice. It may be extremely hard for a junior high school librarian in a heavily Catholic school district to add material describing birth control practices or abortion rights to the collection. Yet, if a social studies curriculum covers these issues, the librarian has an obligation to represent both points of view. Likewise, a public librarian who happens to be gay must acquire materials on both sides of the gay rights issue if he or she is to uphold the Library Bill of Rights. All libraries serve a diverse population, whether or not the diversity is apparent to all members of the community. Such inclusion of viewpoints is essential in realizing the free flow of ideas the First Amendment was created to encourage.

The second sentence in this article—"Materials should not be proscribed or removed because of partisan or doctrinal disapproval"—builds on the inclusivity of the first. Libraries cannot proscriptively exclude materials because some people (school board members, the superintendent, the principal, yes, even the librarian) find them offensive. This article would require us to decline the $10,000 donation for CDs from the board president if accepting it means we can't add rap music because the board president doesn't approve of it. Adherence to this principle is essential if we are to protect the rights of all citizens in the community.

Don't be afraid of new ideas.

Articles 3 and 4

Libraries should challenge censorship in the fulfillment of their responsibility to provide information and enlightenment.

Libraries should cooperate with all persons and groups concerned with resisting abridgment of free expression and free access to ideas.

These articles reflect a sentence from the final paragraph of the "Freedom to Read Statement," a joint statement of the American Library Association and the Association of American Publishers (reprinted in Appendix C): "We believe . . . that what people read is deeply important; that ideas can be dangerous; but that the supression of ideas is fatal to a democratic society."

Libraries are and should be the natural allies of groups that seek to protect civil liberties and the right to receive any and all information. By forming alliances with other groups when they seek to fend off attacks on rights, we both reaffirm our commitment to free and equal access and strengthen a broadly based defense against all attacks on the freedom to read, view, and hear. In the past, application of this article has had librarians forming alliances with publishers, authors, educators, civil libertarians, religious leaders, and others. In the future we will no doubt be forming alliances with those who seek to keep the Internet accessible to all regardless of what content may be on it.

Librarians have a responsibility to challenge censorship because any attempt to restrict what the public has access to lessens our users' ability to make informed and enlightened decisions. Acting on this responsibility is often scary. Chapter 8 offers many practical tips for the librarian faced with a real censorship attempt.

Article 5

A person's right to use a library should not be denied or abridged because of origin, age, background, or views.

This article is the origin of many censorship controversies because it mandates that children be given free access to library collections. While the term *censor* carries with it stereotypical images of angry, less than enlightened people, many (if not most) censorship incidents involve people who truly believe that exposure to "evil" material will corrupt children and destroy the "Christian" or the "American" way of life. Notable exceptions to this generalization include challenges arranged through pressure groups that seek to totally disrupt and take over all segments of the community. The pressure groups and the well-meaning individual have one thing in common: they not only want to control what they and their children have access to, they also want to control what everyone else and their children have access to.

Adherence to this article means that libraries do not adopt policies that set minimum ages for access to materials and equipment with or without parental permission. As stated in ALA's interpretation of the Library Bill of Rights dealing with minors' access to videotapes and other nonprint formats: "Unless directly and specifically prohibited by law from circulating certain motion pictures and video productions to minors, librarians should apply the same standards to circulation of these materials as are applied to books and other material" (see Appendix A for the full text of this and other interpretations). This principle is stated even more explicitly in the ALA's interpretation of the Library Bill of Rights entitled "Free Access to Libraries for Minors":

> Library policies and procedures which effectively deny minors equal access to *all* [emphasis added] library resources available to other users violate the Library Bill of Rights. . . . Librarians and governing authorities should maintain that parents—and only parents—have the right and the responsibility to restrict the access of their children—and only their children—to library resources. Parents or legal guardians who do not want their children to have access to certain library services, materials or facilities, should so advise their children.

In practice, this means that:

- Parents can and should advise their own children on what they consider appropriate for them to read, hear, and view;
- Parents can and should enforce their wishes by dealing directly with their children;
- Parents do not have the right to impose their views on other parents or other people's children;
- Librarians do not and should not have the authority to monitor or restrict any patron's reading; and
- Librarians who set up or adopt "restricted" library cards or practices violate the Library Bill of Rights.

This principle also applies to library fees, as supported by another interpretation of the Library Bill of Rights entitled "Economic Barriers to Information Access." It states that "charging fees for the use of library collections, services, programs, or facilities that were purchased with public funds raises barriers to access. Such fees effectively abridge or deny access for some members of the community because they reinforce distinctions among users based on their ability or willingness to pay." Again, the thread of access to *all* library materials for *all* members of the community is common to intellectual freedom principles and informs the development of all library policies and procedures—even when they don't deal directly with content issues.

Article 6

Libraries which make exhibit spaces and meeting rooms available to the public they serve should make such facilities available on an equitable basis, regardless of the beliefs or affiliations of individuals or groups requesting their use.

This article means that if libraries make exhibit spaces, meeting rooms, or bulletin boards available to community groups, they must ensure that they are available to all groups meeting the stated requirements in an equitable manner. This principle also applies to library-initiated programs such as lectures, community fora, discussion groups, etc. Libraries may not exclude any group based on the subject matter to be discussed or on the ideas that the group advocates. ALA in its interpretations dealing with these topics encourages libraries to clearly define time, place, and manner of use regulations, but discourages qualifications that pertain to the content of a meeting or to the beliefs or affiliations of the sponsors. Such regulations should be stated in inclusive rather than exclusive terms. If libraries choose to limit use of their meeting rooms to "library-related activities," they may do so provided that such activities are viewpoint-neutral.

Interpretations of the Library Bill of Rights

In many ways, the Library Bill of Rights is analogous to the Constitution. It contains short, concise, sharply crafted statements that form a framework within which libraries function, just as our Constitution forms a framework within which our government functions. Just as we do not amend the Constitution each time external circumstances change, ALA does not amend the Library Bill of Rights. ALA instead defines the Library Bill of Rights for changing times through a series of interpretations ranging from "Access for Children and Young People to Videotapes and Other Nonprint Formats: An Interpretation of the Library Bill of Rights" to "Access to Library Resources and Services Regardless of Gender or Sexual Orientation: An Interpretation of the Library Bill of Rights."

These two interpretations are specific examples of how one can take the very short Library Bill of Rights and apply its underlying principles of free and unfettered access to current issues. In the first example, ALA provided an interpretation to explain that the Library Bill of Rights applies to children's right to use videos just as it does to their right to use books. This interpretation makes clear that intellectual freedom's principles apply to access to information regardless of the age of the user or the format of the information. The second example amplified the principle that library resources are for all people and responded to a barrage of censorship incidents involving materials dealing with gay and lesbian issues. To further the constitutional analogy, rather than amending the Library Bill of Rights to include the words *young people*, *videotapes*, *gender*, and *sexual orientation*, ALA simply provided interpretations, just as the courts interpret the Constitution through decisions that spell out how its principles are to be applied.

THE RIGHT TO READ AND PRIVACY

Just as the right to vote can become meaningless without the ballot box's inherent secrecy, the right to read can be meaningless without its inherent right to privacy. Users' right to confidentiality pertains both to their circulation records and to other uses of the library. This basic right to privacy applies as strongly to minors as it does to adults.

Some everyday situations demonstrate why the right to privacy is an essential corollary of the right to read. An employee might be reluctant to inquire at the library about job discrimination or worker's compensation if he has reason to fear that a library employee might gossip about his inquiry and word of his intent might get back to his employer. A teenager might be afraid to check out a book on sex from her school library if her parent could be informed of her reading. An HIV-infected man might avoid reading essential health care information if he was afraid that news of his interest would lead ignorant people to fear contact with him.

While a surface acceptance of users' right to privacy may be easy, implementation of this right throughout library operations and in the face of pressure is, in fact, difficult. Library employees end up explaining to parents that although they may be billed for their children's lost books, they are not entitled to a list of everything their children have checked out. Another difficult enforcement situation might involve inquiries about library use from government or law enforcement agencies.

Concern about library confidentiality exploded, in fact, in 1970 when U.S. Treasury agents visited libraries across the country. These agents visited 27 Atlanta area libraries in one day as well as libraries in other cities at about the same time. In the words of the treasury secretary at the time, the visits were "to determine the advisability of the use of library records as an investigative technique to assist in quelling bombings." ALA's Executive Board issued an emergency advisory statement urging all libraries to make circulation records confidential as a matter of policy. When ALA's Council formally adopted a policy on confidentiality in 1971, David Berninghausen, the chair of the Intellectual Freedom Committee, stated:

> When the time comes in any society that government officials seek information as to what people are reading, it must be presumed that they expect to use these records as evidence of dangerous thinking. . . .
>
> We recognize that the U.S. Treasury agents probably did not realize that their investigations would be viewed as an invasion of privacy of readers or as an infringement on the freedom of thought guaranteed by the U.S. Constitution and Bill of Rights. But it is such small, beginning steps that lead a nation down the road to tyranny (American Library Association 1992, 131).

The issue arose again on a national level in the late 1980s when the FBI's Library Awareness Program came to light (although the program began in the 1960s). FBI agents asked librarians across the country to provide them with information about library use by persons who appeared to be from the Soviet Union or other countries hostile to the U.S. ALA had to educate the agency about the ethical basis for library confidentiality.

Library policies protecting user confidentiality spring from two very different sources: ALA policy (including point 3 in the Statement on Professional Ethics, discussed above) and laws in 45 of the 50 states and the District of Columbia. Ohio, Kentucky, Hawaii, Mississippi, and Utah did not have confidentiality laws as of this writing. Librarians in those states should become familiar with their state's statute.

ALA's policy on confidentiality of library records (ALA Policy 52.4) strongly recommends that the responsible officers of each library in the United States:

1) Formally adopt a policy which specifically recognizes its circulation records and other records identifying the names of library users with specific materials to be confidential.
2) Advise all librarians and library employees that such records shall not be made available to any agency of state, federal, or local government except pursuant to such process, order, or subpoena as may be authorized under the authority of, and pursuant to, federal, state, or local law relating to civil, criminal, or administrative discovery procedures or legislative investigatory power.

FIGURE 1–3 Suggested Procedures for Implementing "Policy on Confidentiality of Library Records"

When drafting local policies, libraries should consult with their legal counsel to insure these policies are based upon and consistent with applicable federal, state, and local law concerning the confidentiality of library records, the disclosure of public records, and the protection of individual privacy.
Suggested procedures include the following:

1. The library staff member receiving the request to examine or obtain information relating to circulation or other records identifying the names of library users, will immediately refer the person making the request to the responsible officer of the institution, who shall explain the confidentiality policy.

2. The director, upon receipt of such process, order, or subpoena, shall consult with the appropriate legal officer assigned to the institution to determine if such process, order, or subpoena is in good form and if there is a showing of good cause for its issuance.

3. If the process, order, or subpoena is not in proper form or if good cause has not been shown, insistence shall be made that such defects be cured before any records are released. (The legal process requiring the production of circulation or other library records shall ordinarily be in the form of subpoena "*duces tecum*" [bring your records] requiring the responsible officer to attend court or the taking of his/her deposition and may require him/her to bring along certain designated circulation or other specified records.)

4. Any threats or unauthorized demands (i.e., those not supported by a process, order, or subpoena) concerning circulation and other records identifying the names of library users shall be reported to the appropriate legal officer of the institution.

5. Any problems relating to the privacy of circulation and other records identifying the names of library users which are not provided for above shall be referred to the responsible officer.

Adopted by the ALA Intellectual Freedom Committee,
January 9, 1983; revised January 11, 1988

Reprinted by permission of the American Library Association

3) Resist the issuance or enforcement of any such process, order, or subpoena until such time as a proper showing of good cause has been made in a court of competent jurisdiction.

ALA's "Policy Concerning Confidentiality of Personally Identifiable Information about Library Users" is reprinted in Appendix A. ALA has also issued suggested procedures for implementing this policy. These procedures are reprinted in figure 1-3.

Librarians follow these principles in order to uphold the rights of the citizens in their community to free and open access to information. The remaining chapters will look at the specifics of ensuring that these principles and rights are honored.

REFERENCE

American Library Association, Office for Intellectual Freedom. *Intellectual Freedom Manual*. 4th ed. Chicago: American Library Association, 1992.

2 LIBRARY POLICIES AND INTELLECTUAL FREEDOM

This chapter defines what policies are, identifies the kinds of policies libraries normally adopt, explores the relationship between policy and procedure, and recommends that all policies be reviewed and adopted by the library's governing authority. A checklist for reviewing existing policies and developing new ones is included. The chapter walks readers through the development of a selection policy and lists criteria that can be used for selection. Selected policies from a variety of libraries are presented from which readers can select parts to be adapted for use in their own policies. The chapter concludes by recommending ways libraries can publicize and promote their policies so as to educate the community and ways they can proactively prevent censorship attempts.

Just as the American Library Association has developed policies to guide the profession concerning intellectual freedom, libraries and their governing boards should develop policies and procedures to provide a framework for implementing the mission and goals of the library, to guide the day-to-day management of the library, and to provide protection from challenges. All policies and procedures follow from the library's mission statement.

WHAT POLICIES DO LIBRARIES HAVE AND WHY SHOULD THEY HAVE THEM?

All libraries have policies, although they don't all have the same policies, nor are they in the same format. Larger libraries tend to have more policies and procedures than small libraries. The intellectual freedom principles introduced in the previous chapter should play key roles in the development and implementation of the following policies on library materials:

- The collection development policy
- The selection policy (criteria)
- The reconsideration policy (which is really a procedure)

Other related policies a library may have are nondiscrimination or human rights policies. School libraries might also be covered by school district policies on academic freedom and selection of academic materials (of which library materials are part). Policies springing from intellectual freedom principles that are specific to public libraries (such as access by minors, meeting rooms, and fees) are covered in chapter 3; policies specific to school libraries are covered in chapter 4. This chapter will consider policies on collection development and materials selection in school and public libraries, since the way these policies are developed and implemented in both settings is similar. The reconsideration policy will be addressed in chapter 6.

One of the most important policies a library has is its collection development policy. This policy includes the library's mission, goals, and objectives. It describes the users and the collection, and it contains sections about the library's commitment to intellectual freedom. The collection development policy also contains sections about the selection and acquisition of materials and reconsideration of challenged materials. One should not confuse a collection development policy with a selection policy. The selection of library material is basically part of library procedures. The policy part may be an introduction to the procedures: who has the legal authority to select and philosophical statements about intellectual freedom and providing a diverse collection. Many libraries, particularly small public libraries and most school libraries, do not have a collection development policy. They have only a selection policy that states what will be acquired and what criteria will be used to select books and other resources.

Many libraries' "policies" are part policy and part procedures. For example, a policy might state that selection is based on reviews in professional resources while a procedure might detail what resources those are. Such a mix can lead to problems during a censorship incident if you find that what you have been calling "policy" does not have the approval of a governing body.

Libraries' policies, particularly collection/selection policies, are critical to guide the library staff and inform the library's users. Most importantly, they can help to protect the library from successful attacks against material in the collection. It is essential to have these policies in place before you need them. When policies and procedures are not in place, librarians are not as successful in fighting attempts to remove items from a collection. Even when policies are in place that provide a bulwark against challenges, people will look for loopholes and try to get library or school boards to make changes.

Policies and procedures can be real life preservers amid troubled waters.

Policies and procedures need to be updated regularly—particularly after any censorship incident or challenge in which the policy is used. Look at the checklist below. Your answers will tell you how much work needs to be done for your library in the policy area.

Policy Review Checklist

- What library policies exist?
- Did you write them and just file them away?
- Is the library staff familiar with the policies?
- If you don't have a collection development policy, have you considered adding one?
- Are your "policies" part policy and part procedure?
- Where are they?
- Have they been approved by a governing body?
- Have they been revised recently?
- Will the policies clearly guide the library through a challenge?
- If you have recently been through a challenge, what worked and what didn't? Did the policy have loopholes?
- Are you providing any "new and different" services, such as access to the Internet? Does this necessitate adding something to your policy?
- Do your policies include an intellectual freedom statement and/or endorsement of ALA's Library Bill of Rights?

DEVELOPING LIBRARY POLICIES

Policy writing is time-consuming and often difficult. Librarians, community members, board members, library users, teachers, and administrators need to be involved in the development and adoption of policy. Involving the community in the preparation of policies can be used to generate goodwill and commitment to the library.

Steps to take before beginning:

- Read the ALA Intellectual Freedom Committee's "Guidelines for the Development and Implementation of Policies, Regulations and Procedures Affecting Access to Library Materials, Services and Facilities" (reprinted in Appendix A).
- Evaluate the current policies of your governing body.
- Decide what needs to be covered, particularly new services or technology like the Internet.
- Decide who is going to draft the initial policies for review.

- Decide what format your policies will take. Will they be short on philosophy and long on procedures? Will there be lengthy philosophical statements? Are procedures included in your policy manual as separate documents, e.g., policies for selection of library materials followed by procedures for selection of library material? Are procedures internal documents only? Do you have one long policy that includes selection, reconsideration, acquisition, weeding, controversial issues, etc., or are these all separate?

There are many ways to write or format policies. A final step before beginning to write a policy is a search of the professional literature for books and articles with examples of collection development and selection policies being used in libraries today. Kay Ann Cassell and Elizabeth Futas's *Developing Public Library Collections, Policies, and Procedures* and Phyllis Van Orden's *The Collection Program in Schools: Concepts, Practices and Information Sources* are good places to start. Many, in fact, most libraries have policies and procedures and share them willingly. You may need to follow a library- or district-wide format. Ideas can also come from sample policies and procedures available from ALA's Office of Intellectual Freedom, the American Association of School Librarians, the Public Library Association, state departments of education, state libraries, and state intellectual freedom committees. Sample policies are tools to use as guides. Read them carefully—you will find many similarities and many differences. Select from those policies statements that meet your needs and the needs of your users.

WHAT SHOULD YOUR POLICY INCLUDE?

Only you can decide what you want in your finished product. The basics include:

- A general philosophical statement regarding the library and its mission
- A description of the user population
- A description of the collection
- A statement of who has the legal authority and responsibility to select materials
- A statement on intellectual freedom
- A statement about network and resource sharing, if appropriate

- A section on selection criteria
- A section on acquisition
- A section on reconsideration

One good way to see what is typically included in collection development policies is to look at the table of contents of several policies. The librarians in the Anchorage (Alaska) School District have drafted a comprehensive document called a Collection Development Policy Statement, which includes the following sections:

- Mission
- Purpose
- Users/Audience
- Brief Overview of Collection
- Assessment
- Selection
- Acquisition
- Access to Materials
    Physical Access
    Intellectual Access
- Deselection
- Reconsideration of Challenged Materials
- Cooperation
- Amendment and Revision

Information Power for Washington, a publication issued by the Washington Library Media Association and the Office of the Washington Superintendent of Public Instruction, suggests that a document for school libraries in Washington State include:

- Philosophy and goals of the school and library media program
- Projected size of the collection
- Systematic review of each category of materials
- Renewal rates for different categories of materials in the collection
- Identification of areas of specialization to meet curricular emphasis and unusual needs
- Criteria for selection of materials
- Criteria to identify materials to be replaced or discarded
- Process to identify user needs and their involvement with selection
- Characteristics of users to be served
- Priorities for acquisition
- Identification of funding sources
- Compilations of a future acquisitions list

The Anchorage School District Collection Development Policy Statement and *Information Power for Washington* include many similar sections. It is not clear from the table of contents where *Information Power for Washington* deals with intellectual freedom issues such as reconsideration of challenged materials.

Cassell and Futas, in *Developing Public Library Collections, Policies, and Procedures,* suggest that a collection development policy include the following sections:

- Mission, goals, objectives
- Community analysis
- Materials selection
- Maintenance
- Evaluation
- Special collections
- Networks, consortiums, cooperation
- Intellectual freedom, censorship, the law

The Cuyahoga County (Ohio) Public Library adopted a different approach. Its policy, on the next page, is widely available to the library's public, is short and philosophical and leaves the details to the library staff. Published as a brochure, it includes ALA's Library Bill of Rights and the library's material selection and access policy. Cuyahoga County's policy, first adopted in 1968, has been reviewed and reaffirmed regularly.

Adopting a Policy

Let's get that one

Cuyahoga County Public Library
Material Selection and Access Policy
(Reprinted with the permission of the Cuyahoga County Public Library)

The Board of Trustees and the Staff of Cuyahoga County Public Library adhere to the American Library Association Bill of Rights.

WHICH IDEAS WILL BE REPRESENTED IN THE LIBRARY?

The public library is the institution in our society which provides material representing all points of view in all fields, including political, social, and religious, no matter how controversial or how objectionable these ideas may be to some people. In a democratic society, individuals should feel free to explore any and all ideas in order to decide which are meaningful to them. Therefore, the library, within the limits of selections standards, budget, and space, chooses representative material espousing all points of view.

FOR WHAT PURPOSE IS LIBRARY MATERIAL SELECTED?

The primary objective of the public library is to serve as a communications center for the total community by providing free and open access to the ideas and information available on all subjects and in all media. Cuyahoga County Public Library selects and makes available material for the enlightenment, cultural development, and enjoyment of its public at all ages and levels of ability and interest. All materials are available to all.

HOW DOES THE LIBRARY SELECT SOME MATERIAL AND NOT OTHERS?

Budgetary and space constraints limit all libraries' ability to purchase material. Therefore, qualitative selection standards have been developed by specialists in adults, young adult, juvenile, and audiovisual services. Librarians evaluate material on the basis of these standards and recommendations from acceptable professional and commercial reviews. Popularity and community demand are among the major criteria for selecting materials. Consideration is given to material which may be of interest to a few patrons as well as that of interest to many patrons. Under a cooperative program, Cuyahoga County Public Library obtains, through inter-library loan, material owned by other libraries.

In accordance with the American Library Association's Library Bill of Rights, materials on controversial subjects or issues, even if presented in an extreme or sensational manner, are acquired.

You might ask: "So Anchorage does this, Cassell and Futas recommend that, and Cuyahoga County does yet something else. What should we do?" This book can't dictate what you should do. Instead, it looks at the usefulness of policies for you and your patrons and presents an array of especially sound policies from which you can choose elements that will best meet your needs.

LIBRARY POLICIES AND THE INTERNET

As more and more libraries offer access to the Internet, library directors, library boards, school librarians, and school boards are seeing a need to include statements about intellectual freedom and the Internet in their policies. This may take the form of a new policy or of an amendment to existing policies. The American Library Association was developing an interpretation of the Library Bill of Rights dealing with access to electronic information, services, and networks as this book was being written. In the absence of an ALA policy at this time, we can look at the policies developed by several libraries around the country.

The Montgomery-Floyd Regional Library in Virginia offers free Internet access to the public via the Blacksburg Electronic Village. Knowing that offering access to the Internet often raises intellectual freedom issues, the library board decided to be proactive. A 1994 computer use policy states, in part: "The same standards of intellectual freedom, privacy, and confidentiality endorsed by the American Library Association and incorporated in Montgomery-Floyd Regional Library Policies for traditional media shall be applied to all electronic media." A statement is given to patrons who apply for e-mail accounts that reads, "Please be aware that some information found on the Internet is of a mature nature, and may not be suitable for your children. **Parents or guardians, not the library or its staff, are responsible for the information selected and/or accessed by children.**"

The St. Joseph County [Indiana] Public Library, one of the first public libraries with a World Wide Web site, keeps a listing of all public libraries with Internet access. St. Joseph recently added onto its selection and collection development policies an Internet policy. The St. Joseph County Public Library Computer Usage Policy and Disclaimer includes the following language: "Since the Internet is a global electronic network, there is no state/county control of its users or content. The Internet and its available resources may contain material of a controversial nature. The Library cannot censor access to material nor protect users from offensive information. Parents of minor children must assume responsibility for their children's use of the Internet through the Library's connection."

To help librarians, the American Library Association maintains a World Wide Web home page [http://.www.ala.org]. ALA's web page contains many valuable intellectual freedom resources.

THE SELECTION POLICY

When librarians select materials to add to their collections, they necessarily exclude others. They are often asked, particularly during a censorship incident, what makes them different from censors.

In 1953 Lester Asheim wrote what is now a classic article published in *Wilson Library Bulletin*, "Not Censorship but Selection," which outlines the differences between selection and censorship:

> The major characteristics which make for the all-important difference seems to be this: that the selector's approach is positive, while that of the censor is negative. For the selector, the important thing is to find reasons to keep the book. Given such a guiding principle, the selector looks for values, for strengths, for virtues which will overshadow minor objections. For the censor . . . the important thing is to find reasons to reject the book; his guiding principle leads him to seek out the objectionable feature, the weaknesses, the possibilities for misinterpretation.
>
> Selection's approach to the book is positive, seeking its values in the book as a book, and in the book as a whole. Censorship's approach is negative, seeking for vulnerable characteristics wherever they can be found—anywhere within the book; or even outside it. Selection seeks to protect the right of the reader to read; censorship seeks to protect—not that right—but the reader himself from the fancied effects of his reading. The selector has faith in the intelligence of the reader; the censor has faith only in his own. The aim of the selector is to promote reading, not to inhibit it (Asheim 1953, 66–67).

Selecting materials is one of the most important and interesting jobs a librarian has. It is also time-consuming, and as technology provides us with more and varied formats, this task has become more and more complex. In order to perform the job of selecting resources, libraries must adopt selection criteria. These criteria are the most important part of the selection policy. They must be applied to donated as well as to purchased materials. The selection "policy" (or procedure) and criteria are a guide. No single standard exists which can be applied in all selection decisions. Some materials are judged for their literary merit, others for artistic merit, and cost may be a factor when judging others. Some items are chosen because they meet the educational needs of patrons while some are chosen solely because of anticipated demand, or because they support the school curriculum. The collection in total should represent, as much as possible, the needs of all users.

Key items in a selection document should include:

- Legal responsibility for selection
- Balance/diversity, controversial issues
- Selection criteria
- Criteria for discarding, weeding, or deselecting
- Reconsideration process

STANDARD SELECTION CRITERIA

Many selection documents list general criteria for selection, sometimes broken down into categories: fiction, nonfiction, and media. The same general criteria are seen over and over in many selection documents; almost like public domain software, they seem to get passed around the country and used in libraries until nobody can remember who first wrote them. Some documents elaborate on what each item means and some do not. If you choose to list only "one-word" criteria, such as "accuracy" or "demand," in your policy/procedures, be sure that you are able to define them. Don't find yourself with written criteria you have picked up from lists but that you can't explain to other librarians, your administration, the board, or parents.

There is a thin line between censorship and selection

Criteria to select from for your own list might include:

- Accessibility to the title through indexes and bibliographies
- Accuracy of information
- Appropriate depth of coverage of topics to suit patrons' needs, reading level
- Appropriate writing style or presentation to suit the audience
- Appropriateness and effectiveness of the medium to the content
- Appropriateness of content to users
- Attention from critics, reviewers, and public
- Audience for material
- Author's credentials
- Authoritativeness and honesty
- Authority, effectiveness, timeliness of presentation
- Authority, skill, competence, reputation, and significance of the author
- Availability and accessibility of the same materials locally
- Availability of materials elsewhere in the region or through interlibrary loan
- Budgetary limitations
- Clarity, accuracy, logic, objectivity, and readability
- Collection objectives
- Composition of present collection
- Comprehensiveness and depth of treatment
- Contemporary or permanent value
- Contribution of work toward balanced collection representing a broad range of perspectives and opinions, including extreme and/or minority points of view
- Creativity
- Critics' and staff members' reviews
- Cultural diversity of the school community
- Cultural, recreational, information, and/or educational value
- Current or historical significance of author or subject
- Curriculum needs of students and teachers
- Demand for the material
- Diversity of viewpoint
- Durability of information
- Educational significance
- Funds and space

- Imaginative quality
- Importance as a document of the time
- Importance of the subject matter
- Insight into human and social conditions
- Need for duplicate materials in the existing collection
- Objectivity and integrity
- Patron requests
- Personal and recreational needs of students
- Physical and developmental stages of students
- Popularity as measured by *New York Times Book Review* best-sellers, Christian retailing top sellers, or other such lists
- Potential use
- Present and potential relevance to community needs
- Price
- Public demand
- Public interest
- Publisher's reputation
- Quality of the physical format
- Reading enjoyment
- Relationship to existing materials in the collection on the same subject
- Representation of challenging, though extreme or minority, points of view
- Reputation of author, artist, or producer
- Social significance
- Space limitations
- Subject coverage to fill needs in the collection
- Suitability of content and style for intended audience
- Suitability of physical form for library use
- Suitability of subject, style, and reading level for intended audience
- Supports the curriculum
- Timeliness or permanence of topic
- Treatment, arrangement, and organization
- Unique characteristics of the local community
- Value to the collection
- Varying points of view and opinions

The above list is *very* long: it illustrates the variety and depth of choices librarians have. There is no one true list of selection criteria that works for every library. You may be in a small specialized library serving students in a magnet theater program, a public library serving a community of 2,000, a branch of a suburban system, an inner-city branch of an urban system, a central resource facility, or a very large college prep high school. Each librarian needs to decide for him or herself which criteria meet the needs of the library's users.

If you are providing access to the Internet and link material from the electronic universe to make it easily available to patrons on your own library's home page, will you use the same criteria, or will they be different? The Berkeley (California) Public Library provides an index to the Internet that changes weekly as new resources are added. Carol Leita, BPL's Internet librarian, uses the following basic criteria when looking for items to add to the Berkeley index: authority of source, currentness (when appropriate), stability, and interest to public library patrons.

BIAS IN SELECTION

Librarians must address, personally and professionally, the topic of bias in selection. *Internal censorship*, *voluntary censorship*, *silent censors*, and *pre-* and *post-selection censorship* are a few of the other names this goes by. Are your biases showing in your collection?

This type of censorship does occur, probably more frequently than librarians would like to admit. It happens when librarians remove or restrict library material or do not purchase certain titles, perhaps as a result of pressure from school administrators, the city manager, board members, or members of the community. The pressure to remove, restrict, or not purchase material may be real, or the librarian may be anxious about future consequences. After a censorship incident in a community, whether the book is retained or not, many librarians tend not to want to repeat the experience. School boards and administrators are definitely not anxious to have their time consumed by challenges. The "chilling effect" comes into play when it is easier not to purchase something controversial, even when it meets selection criteria, than to risk having a selection decision challenged.

Frances Jones in *Defusing Censorship* is very specific about censorship by libraries. She says, "Preselection censorship occurs when works are not selected because they are controversial in the opinion of library selectors; when too few copies of a controversial work are purchased to meet the demand for them; when reviews do not appear in the most frequently consulted review sources; when materials are selected for the collection because of their subjects or formats; and when specific categories of materials are not selected because of the selector's belief that the library users lack background to use or appreciate them" (Jones 1983, 117–118). Another form of censorship is when librarians pass up materials from small presses because they are not familiar with the publisher or do not take the time to seek out small press material.

In addition to issues of bias in the selection process, there are other internal practices that run counter to intellectual freedom principles. They are defined in the ALA interpretations of the Library Bill of Rights. According to ALA, labeling materials "by affixing a prejudicial label and/or segregating them by a prejudicial system" is one form of internal censorship practice. Another, more common than we like to think, is restricting use of materials, particularly by young patrons. A third is expurgation. The ALA OIF manual defines this as "any deletion, excision, alteration, or obliteration of any part(s) of a book or other library resources by the library." The swimsuit issue of *Sports Illustrated* has been subjected to expurgation in recent times. In both 1994 and 1995 librarians on LM_NET, a listserv for school librarians, reported ways in which the magazine was altered in libraries— cutting out the "offending" pages, gluing them together, "losing" the issue before it went out on the shelf.

Your library should have something to offend everybody—including you, even if it's the swimsuit issues of *Sports Illustrated*. Personal views should not be the basis for selection or removal decisions. Are you aware of your biases? Does your collection reflect a wide variety of views? Are you the only person in the library doing selection? Who else has input into the selection process? Can a person look at a section of the library—such as the area on abortion—and tell where you stand on this issue?

Problems created by internal censorship are scary because we expect members of the library profession to follow the basic tenets of the profession, and intellectual freedom is one of the most basic. These problems can be solved, however, because, unlike challenges that are external, these problems are basically in the library's control. In *Defusing Censorship*, Jones provides guidelines for dealing with the problem, including recognizing the possibility of internal censorship, dealing with conflict on the library staff, creating an open workplace that incorporates staff training, and supplementing selection policies with appropriate procedures.

OTHER PARTS OF THE POLICIES/PROCEDURES

Selection and the criteria for selecting materials may be an important part of the policies and procedures you write, but they are by no means the only part. Other major sections of your policy/procedures will include:

- Acquisitions
- Reconsideration
- Weeding
- Review of the policy

Reconsideration is such an important part of the document in terms of dealing with censorship that it will be covered by itself in chapter 6.

Whatever format your policies take, bring all policies and procedures pertaining to the library's collection together in one place so that you and your users have ready access to them. Check to be sure they form a cohesive work reflecting the library's commitment to intellectual freedom and to serving all of its constituency.

APPROVAL OF POLICIES

For policies to be beneficial to the library, particularly when fighting censorship, they must be approved by a governing body that has the authority to set policy. Writing a selection policy and sticking it in your drawer is better than nothing, but not much if you are involved in a full-blown censorship incident. Not only will you find yourself defending the book (or other material) but you will also be defending your authority to speak on behalf of your governing body. This is particularly true in school districts where you may be the only professional librarian for miles.

When policies are to be considered by governing bodies, generally public notice must be given in accordance with local or state law. Public comment may also be requested prior to approval when policies are in draft form. If you have concerns about anything in the policies of the library or school district being approved, voice them in writing or in person. Many bureaucracies require that contact with the governing board be made through the superintendent or library director; some do not. Find a way to speak directly to the board. Don't assume anyone else is going to speak for intellectual freedom principles, especially at the school board level—and don't assume that you will get "in trouble" if you speak. At a school board meeting you may testify as a parent or as a community member. You do not have to testify as an employee. The same is true before a library board. Don't ever abrogate your right to speak in a public forum. If you feel uncomfortable or think there is trouble ahead for you, find parents, concerned citizens, or librarians from other libraries to speak. Parents who have problems with the library's policies about youth access will certainly be there to testify and often ask board members to pass policies that require the library to restrict access for their children. Do not get caught by surprise. Attend school board meetings, especially when there is policy under consideration that affects the library's program. Ask that the governing board adopt the Library Bill of Rights as part of the policies.

If you work in a school district where you think the policies need improving, or there are no policies at all, work with the district's library coordinator, the assistant superintendent, or whomever oversees the school library media program. Boards generally do not write their own policies; they ask management to do it for them to review and approve. You can become a part of the process before it ever gets to the approval stage.

If you work in a library that has an advisory, instead of a governing, board, you will need to have your general political body (county assembly, city council, etc.) approve part or all of your policy. Because there is a strong possibility that political pressures unrelated to the library may cause problems in a general body, plan your approach carefully. One tactic is to assume that selection of materials is an administrative function delegated by the mayor or city manager and address only the reconsideration procedure. Whether or not you address selection, the reconsideration procedure should be adopted to give you the strongest support for handling challenges to the collection.

Procedures are generally written after policies are approved. They may be written as a companion piece to policies so that a governing board has the opportunity to look at policy and management's procedures at the same time. While governing bodies do not adopt procedures, there may be times when they want to comment on procedures and may, in fact, ask management to revise them.

WHAT TO DO WITH POLICIES AFTER APPROVAL

Your policies are approved! The next step is to ensure that there are procedures in place that match your policies. You have them all in one place in a folder along with your reconsideration form. You are all set—you never have to think about them again—until a parent comes through the door to discuss a book he or she finds objectionable. Right? WRONG! Unfortunately, now your work begins in another arena: public awareness about intellectual freedom.

Libraries, large and small, should have a plan to promote themselves, their policies, and their services, and the most important service that libraries provide is access to information and protection of the right to read across the total spectrum of ideas and beliefs. Isn't that what your policies say? Don't libraries protect the public's interest? Isn't the library the one public institution that provides materials and information representing all points of view without endorsing the viewpoint of the material or the author? It's difficult to promote a policy, but easy to promote a concept.

Doing everything right does not guarantee a career free of censorship incidents. You have policies and procedures. They are approved. You select diverse materials to meet the needs of your users. You promote intellectual freedom; you attend workshops. And when the censor walks in the door your heart almost stops beating—but you are prepared.

REFERENCES

American Library Association, Office for Intellectual Freedom. *Intellectual Freedom Manual.* 4th ed. Chicago: American Library Association, 1992.

Anchorage (Alaska) School District. "Collection Development Policy Statement for the Anchorage School District" Draft document, Anchorage, AK: Anchorage School District, 1992.

Asheim, Lester. "Not Censorship but Selection." *Wilson Library Bulletin* (September 1953).

Cassell, Kay Ann, and Elizabeth Futas. *Developing Public Library Collections, Policies, and Procedures: A How-To-Do-It Manual for Small and Medium Sized Public Libraries.* New York: Neal-Schuman Publishers, 1991.

Helm, Steven P. (shelm@vt.edu). Kids and Internet FYI [(posting to ALAOIF)]. January 29, 1995.

Jones, Frances M. *Defusing Censorship: The Librarian's Guide to Handling Censorship Conflicts*. Phoenix, AZ: Oryx Press, 1983.

Montgomery-Floyd (Virginia) Regional Library. "Montgomery-Floyd Regional Library Computer Use Policy," 1994.

St. Joseph County (Indiana) Public Library. "St. Joseph County Public Library Computer Usage Policy and Disclaimer," 1995.

Van Orden, Phyllis. *The Collection Program in Schools: Concepts, Practices and Information Sources*. Englewood, CO: Libraries Unlimited. 1988.

Washington Library Media Association. Standards Committee. *Information Power for Washington; Guidelines for School Library Media Programs*. Rev. 1991. Olympia, WA: Office of Superintendent of Public Instruction, 1991.

3 CONSIDERATIONS SPECIFIC TO PUBLIC LIBRARIES

If this nation is to be wise as well as strong, if we are to achieve our destiny, then we need more ideas for more wise men reading more good books in more public libraries. These libraries should be open to all—except the censor. We must know all the facts and hear all the alternatives and listen to all the criticisms. Let us welcome controversial books and controversial authors. For the Bill of Rights is the guardian of our security as well as our Library.

John F. Kennedy as quoted in
ALA's Intellectual Freedom Manual

The unique, open nature of the public library presents special considerations for policy development and implementation. This chapter looks at the governance of public libraries, explores appropriate and inappropriate roles for trustees to play in library operations, and presents tips for working with trustees on matters pertaining to intellectual freedom. Specific areas of discussion include access issues, exhibits, bulletin boards, programming, meeting rooms, and fees.

In upholding intellectual freedom principles, public libraries operate within a much wider venue than do school, special, and academic libraries. This wider venue is a natural by-product of the much broader public library mission statement. Whereas other types of libraries serve a very defined—indeed closed—community, public libraries serve the entirety of the community. Figure 3-1 illustrates this overlap.

WHO GOVERNS AND WHO MANAGES PUBLIC LIBRARIES?

According to *The ALA Glossary of Library and Information Science*, a public library is:

any library which provides general library services without charge to all residents of a given community, district, or region. Supported by public or private funds, the public library makes its basic collections and basic services available to the population of its legal service area without charges to individual users, but may impose charges on users outside its legal service area. Products and services beyond the library's basic services may or may not be provided to the public at large and may or may not be provided without individual charges (Young 1983).

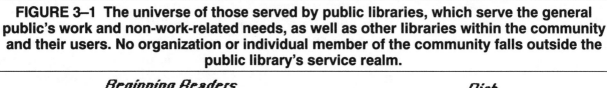

FIGURE 3–1 The universe of those served by public libraries, which serve the general public's work and non-work-related needs, as well as other libraries within the community and their users. No organization or individual member of the community falls outside the public library's service realm.

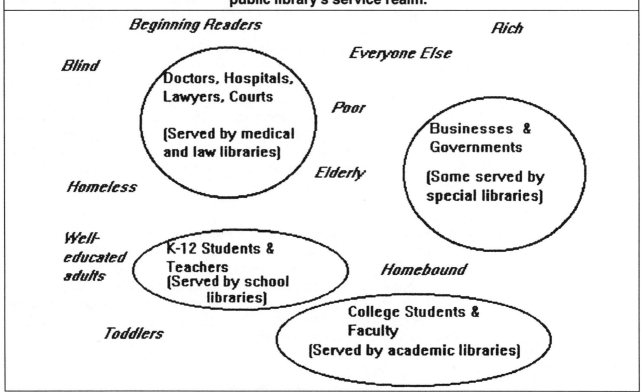

According to the latest government statistics, there were 8,946 U.S. public libraries in 1992 (National Center for Education Statistics 1994, 17). As listed in the 1994 edition of *The Public Library Data Service Statistical Report,* these libraries range in size from Idaho's Salmon River Public Library, which serves 428 people, to the Los Angeles Public Library, which serves 3,500,000 people. Although the staffing of these two libraries is as different as the numbers and types of people they serve, both libraries have the same *raison d'être:* to do the best jobs they can of meeting the reading, viewing, listening, and informational needs of those in their communities.

By law, most public libraries are governed by a board of trustees (some public library boards are more "advisory" than "governing"). Members of these boards are either appointed by a governing body or official (73.2 percent) or elected (26.8 percent) (Arney 1988, 2). Trustees have a number of duties, including hiring a director, adopting policies (including those dealing with book and materials selection), determining the library's mission, approving a budget, and reporting regularly to the governing officials and general public.

Many small public libraries are staffed by volunteers. Other public libraries have part-time or full-time staff without formal library education; these staff members usually have participated in library training workshops run by regional or state library agencies. Generally, public libraries serving populations larger than 20,000 employ a professional librarian (meaning a librarian with an ALA-accredited master's degree in library and information studies). Whether the public library is run by a volunteer, a high school graduate, or a director assisted by 100 M.L.S. librarians, if there is a board of trustees, the librarian usually develops and recommends policies. It is the board of trustees, representing the community's public, who approves these policies. In doing so, the trustees both ensure that the community's wishes are carried out and support the librarian as he or she carries out board-approved policies in the performance of day-to-day operations.

THE TRUSTEE AS PROTECTOR OF FREE AND OPEN ACCESS

Trustees play an essential role in protecting the public's right to free and open access to information through the library. In fact, Judith F. Krug (director of ALA's Office for Intellectual Freedom) and Alex P. Allain (a trustee from Louisiana and the Freedom to Read Foundation's first president) once wrote that:

> If access to and availability of information are the key words underscoring the unique role libraries play in the functioning of our democracy, it is no less a truism to say that it is the trustee's commitment to intellectual freedom, reflected in the

policies established and the support provided for implementation of these policies, that allows the concept of intellectual freedom to flourish (Krug 1988, 135).

In developing and approving policies governing collection development, selection, reconsideration, and other access issues, trustees, like librarians, must realize that some decisions will be controversial. In the best of all possible worlds, trustees will support both each other and the librarian in developing and implementing these policies, while guarding against internal censorship as diligently as they guard against external censorship. Just as the librarian should not let his or her own personal tastes and preferences influence selection decisions, trustees should make sure that their perspectives do not pervade policy and program development.

In guarding free and open access to information, trustees

(1) Hire the person they believe will best serve their community as the library director;
(2) Work with that person to either devise or revise collection development and other library policies;
(3) Ultimately approve these policies;
(4) Delegate to the librarian the responsibility for materials selection and collection development within the framework of those policies; and
(5) Accept responsibility and ownership, along with that librarian, for the collection's content.

It is essential that the trustees and the librarian support each other throughout all five steps.

Because they usually hire and fire the librarian, it is ultimately the trustees who stand between the library and those who would seek to impose their beliefs and values on others. How, then, do public librarians prepare trustees for censorship attempts?

EDUCATION AND PREPARATION EQUAL SUCCESS

More trustees may come to libraries because of a love of libraries and their ability to be advocates for funding and/or political support than because of their knowledge of First Amendment principles or practices. One of the first activities librarians should engage in with newly elected trustees is an educational process about the general principles of library service and the individual library's policies and procedures. While this orientation will necessarily cover a wide variety of topics such as the physical state of the library building, budget matters, and parliamentary procedure, we will focus here on matters affecting intellectual freedom.

Whether the orientation process is formal or informal, it should be consciously planned, developed, and carried out. Trustees who perceive themselves being treated as rubber stamps for whatever the librarian wants will be of little help when there's a real disagreement about a controversial issue, much less when the community erupts in a censorship battle and calls for the librarian to be fired. Achieving this understanding may mean undertaking one-on-one talks, participating in board retreats, attending regional and state workshops as well as ALA conferences, and reading and discussing books and articles developed for library trustees. Librarians should encourage all their trustees to join ALA and the American Library Trustee Association (ALTA), an ALA division devoted to the concerns of library trustees, as well as their state library association. Interaction on a national and regional level can be a powerful support mechanism for trustees and is one of the few opportunities trustees have to get to know and form alliances with trustees from other libraries. Not only will such interaction be useful in an intellectual freedom context, it will also bolster all aspects of the total library program. Whatever combination of methods is used, it is essential that an understanding of intellectual freedom be achieved *before* trustees are placed in the position of having to defend it in their library.

The books in your library are documents of the times

THE TRUSTEE AND THE COLLECTION

Trustees approve collection development and selection policies. These policies should describe how the collection realizes the library's mission and the criteria used for selecting materials for acquisition. They give the board a tool by which both to evaluate the collection and to explain what the library is all about to the community. The board can also use these policies in educating community members so that citizens understand what the library does.

Citizens sometimes ask board members, "But don't you approve selection decisions?" This question may lead trustees to ask each other and the library director if they should get involved in the selection process. The answer to both these questions is "no." Boards make policy; they don't implement it. Selection decisions are implementation decisions. Lorraine Williams sums the distinction up quite well when she says:

> Trustees put themselves in an impossible situation by getting involved in book selection. It is stepping over the line between making policy and administering policy. The librarian and staff are trained in that discipline or, if not, can obtain the necessary professional help to insure well-rounded collections. Trustees are free to make suggestions about books that should be added to the system, but their recommendations should be given no more or less weight than those of any other patron making such a request. Nor is it binding on the staff to purchase every book that is suggested, regardless of who makes the suggestion (Williams 1993, 120).

It behooves the librarian to make sure all members of the board understand and accept the interrelationships inherent between these three levels:

1. Principles: key documents like the Library Bill of Rights;
2. Local library restatement and adoption of principles (statements like the library's own selection and collection development policies); and
3. Practice: each and every selection decision as an implementation of both (1) and (2).

Williams elegantly summarizes the gap between knee-jerk lip service to the Library Bill of Rights and defending the controversial selection decision as follows: "Intellectual freedom is one of the most attractive principles for fair-minded people to support in theory; in practice it is one of the hardest to abide by" (Williams 1993, 126). It's every bit as crucial that religious trustees be willing to accept that atheist magazines might be available in "their" library as it is that the most secular trustee accept that books advocating religion as a "treatment" for homosexuality have an audience among some segment of the community. Here again, librarians, library users, and library trustees must all be willing to be offended by something in the library.

ACCESS TO PUBLIC LIBRARIES

Up to this point, this chapter has focused on what is in the collection: the people and policies that determine what is acquired and what is not. This section will look at what determines who gets to *use* those materials once they are selected, acquired, cataloged, and available.

As stated in chapter 1, the Library Bill of Rights and its interpretations vigorously uphold the rights of all people to use all parts of the library and to avail themselves of all library services. Article five—"A person's right to use a library should not be denied or abridged because of origin, age, background or views"—clearly demands unlimited access for all. Article six—"Libraries which make exhibit spaces and meeting rooms available to the public they serve should make such facilities available on an equitable basis, regardless of the beliefs or affiliations of individuals or groups requesting their use"—extends this access to the very public arenas of art displays, programming, and public meetings held on library grounds.

Citizens naturally feel that because public libraries are supported with their tax dollars that they should have some say in how those dollars are spent and in the rules and regulations governing the use of public facilities. One of the most important ways to protect the right to read, listen, and view is to remind citizens who take exception to a specific title or event that: (1) the First Amendment guarantees people's right to receive information; (2) the library serves all people and that Mr. or Ms. X doesn't have to check out the title in question or attend the program and that there are lots of other materials available that he or she does approve of and like; and (3) they do indeed have a voice and representation in how the library is run through the library's board of trustees, which represents the public (including Mr. or Ms. X).

Appendix A includes reprints of interpretations of the Library Bill of Rights. Key ones affecting principles of access in public libraries are: "Restricted Access to Library Materials," "Statement on Labeling," "Access for Children and Young People to Videotapes and Other Nonprint Formats," "Access to Library Resources and Services Regardless of Gender or Sexual Orientation," "Free Access to Libraries for Minors," "Economic Barriers to Information Access," "Exhibit Spaces and Bulletin Boards," and "Meeting Rooms." Public libraries should review their policies and procedures to make sure that (1) existing policies and procedures are not in conflict with these interpretations and (2) all the rights called for in these ALA statements are guaranteed to the library's patrons through board-approved policies. By taking a proactive approach to policy development *before* a controversial situation arises, librarians and trustees can both ensure that the public's rights are protected and save themselves from having to develop policies in the media spotlight and in reaction to uncomfortable situations.

To help libraries carry out this policy development, the American Library Association recently issued "Guidelines for the Development and Implementation of Policies, Regulations and Procedures Affecting Access to Library Materials, Services and Facilities," reprinted in Appendix A. Because they highlight the interrelationships between various sources such as the Constitution, the Library Bill of Rights, and individual library policies, the guidelines offer libraries a perspective in which to frame rules and regulations affecting access as well as practical guidance for reviewing and developing such rules and regulations. Of paramount philosophical importance for most libraries are guidelines four (calling for rules/regulations to be based upon the library's mission and objectives) and six (requiring that such rules should not be more restrictive than needed to serve their objectives).

Most controversies over public library access policies involve what areas of the library and what materials are accessible to children. Many good-hearted people feel that if children just did not know about sex, drugs, violence, etc., they would be better off. In response to these comments, library policy must say that every parent has the right—indeed the responsibility—to guide his or her child's reading, viewing, etc., but *only* his or her child's. One parent or citizen does not have the right or the responsibility to control what any other child or any other person has access to. To control anyone else's, or anyone else's child's reading, would be antithetical to our country's foundation in freedom and liberty.

Many libraries have developed excellent public relations tools to explain this freedom to parents who might have concerns about what their child or other children have access to in the library. The most difficult moment in dealing with these encounters arises when a parent nods politely as the librarian explains that he or she cannot restrict the child's reading and then says, "Oh, but I just want you to make sure little Betsy doesn't get in the sex books." When that happens, libraries need to have something ready that clearly explains the board-approved policies to the citizen. Excerpts from some excellent brochures follow. These can be adapted for local library use.

A Seattle Public Library handout entitled "Dear Parent or Guardian" contains this paragraph: "You should be aware that library policy permits all children access to all materials in the system. As a parent or guardian, if you desire to limit your child's access to library materials, you should make this desire known to your child. The library cannot withhold circulating materials from any patron, regardless of age" (Seattle Public Library 1982).

The Michigan Library Association's Intellectual Freedom Committee developed a pamphlet entitled "Some Words for the Concerned Citizen" (Michigan Library Association 1982). It includes these two points:

> We cannot bar some persons from some parts of the collection on the basis of their age, sex, viewpoint, or another factor. You would be justifiably angry if we refused to collect and loan materials in which you had great interest or for which you had a need because you were too young, or of a particular religion, background, or viewpoint.
>
> We encourage children and young people to use the library. However the library does not have the legal right to act *in loco parentis* (in place of the parent). Therefore, if you are concerned that your children might bring home a book which does not meet your personal standards, please accompany them when they use the collection. We are not free to forbid your children to read anything, but you are as their parent. Our staff will be glad to help you and your children make suitable decisions.

The Freedom to Read Committee of the Association of American Publishers has a brochure entitled "Books and the Young Reader: A Statement for Communities, Schools and Libraries" containing these two excellent sentences: "What one parent will approve of for a child, another will not. The rights of one parent to provide a child with the materials that parent finds acceptable should not be abridged by the views of another" (Association of American Publishers).

These statements clearly uphold the rights of children to use libraries without restriction. They communicate this right with respect both for the children and for the views of individual parents who may wish to restrict their own children's reading. The tone of all three samples resounds with the clear (and hard to criticize) ring of patriotism. Libraries seeking more information about children's rights and the language to use to communicate these rights are especially referred to two interpretations of the Library Bill of Rights, "Free Access to Libraries for Minors" and "Access for Children and Young People to Videotapes and Other Nonprint Formats." Both are reprinted in Appendix A.

EXHIBITS, BULLETIN BOARDS, PROGRAMMING, AND MEETING ROOMS

Books, videotapes, recorded music, CD-ROM databases, and magazines are tangible, inert materials. Almost everyone accepts that these collections are a given part of library services. However, some of the most visible aspects of library programs are transitory. Special library programming such as lectures, film series, art exhibits, and meetings held on library property often garner special media attention and, if controversial, can become *causes célèbres* in the community.

As with other aspects of library service, it is essential that the library have well-written, comprehensive policies governing the administration of these events. It is equally important that, once these policies are adopted, the procedures used to implement them are applied consistently and equally. If the library, for example, routinely lets one group book a meeting room at the spur of the moment with a phone call and then requires a second group to fill out three forms and post an insurance bond, the library not only invites a public relations problem but also opens itself to potential litigation.

You, your staff, and your public must view policies as statements that guide everyday administration and use of the library, not as pages to be filed in a dusty notebook that is referred to only when there's an unpleasant situation or controversy brewing. A very wise library director once said, "It's just as important that every circulation clerk understand our policies and procedures as it is that I understand them." These words are all the more true because it is frontline staff who first get asked about and usually carry out the policies, whether the policies govern who gets a library card or who can display their collection of stamps, coins, pastoral watercolors, or erotic statuary in the library's front hall.

ALA has adopted interpretations of the Library Bill of Rights covering all these areas. They are reprinted in Appendix A. Key concepts include:

Exhibit Spaces
- If made available to the public, they should be administered without regard to the beliefs or affiliations of those requesting their use.
- In developing exhibits, staff should endeavor to present a broad spectrum of opinion.
- A publicly supported library *may* limit use of its exhibit space to strictly "library-related" activities *if* that limitation is clearly circumscribed and is viewpoint-neutral.
- Any rules must be applied to everyone.

Bulletin Boards
- If bulletin boards are made available to the public, libraries should develop use criteria similar to those discussed above for exhibits.
- Bulletin board criteria may also address the size of material to be displayed, the length of time materials may remain posted, the frequency with which material may be posted for the same group, and the geographic area from which notices will be accepted.

Meeting Rooms
- If made available to the public, they should be administered without regard to the beliefs or affiliations of those requesting their use.
- Libraries should develop and publish policy statements governing their use.
- If meeting rooms in public libraries are made available to the general public for non-library sponsored events, the library may not exclude *any* group based on the subject matter to be discussed.
- Libraries may want to post a permanent notice near meeting rooms stating that the library does not advocate or

endorse the viewpoints of meetings or meeting room users.

Programming

- Library-initiated programs in libraries serving multilingual or multicultural communities make efforts to accommodate those for whom English is a second language.
- Programming should not be proscribed or removed (canceled) because of those who may disapprove of the contents.
- Library-initiated programs are library resources and, like all resources, are developed in accordance with written guidelines approved and adopted by the library's board.
- Programs are developed based on the interests and information needs of the community served.

DO FEES INFRINGE UPON INTELLECTUAL FREEDOM?

Obviously, it does no good for the library to acquire, collect, organize, or otherwise provide access to information if users cannot access that information. Because of public libraries' mission to serve all citizens of the community, their services have traditionally been free. With the advent of inexpensive, easy-to-use photocopying, all types of libraries began charging fees for duplication services. The rationale for these charges was that people could still use the library's resources, take notes, and/or copy information in longhand without any charge. Any nominal fee charged (five, ten, or fifteen cents per page) simply offset the additional costs (such as consumable supplies) of making copies convenient for patrons to make. After all, librarians reasoned, if patrons checked the books out and took them to a commercial service or their office to copy them, they would still have to pay and it would be less convenient.

When university libraries began searching expensive online databases for faculty and students, many of them also extended this "pass-along" principle to charges incurred for database services. Public libraries faced a real dilemma when they began considering providing access to these same databases: if they could not afford to underwrite search costs, they either had to charge patrons for some or all of the search costs or not provide access to the services, thus, in effect, offering less than state-of-the-art information access. With the convergence of spiraling materials costs, unprecedented increases in the popularity of information technology, and the economics of the 1980s and 1990s (the recession, government downsizing, and tax revolts), more and more public libraries began charging for one type of service or another. In fact, a 1993 survey by the Urban Libraries Council showed that 98 percent of urban libraries charged for photocopies, 57 percent charged for online searching, 14 percent charged patrons to check out a video, 24 percent charged patrons for interlibrary loans of materials their library did not own, and 2 percent even charged patrons to check out books on tape (Urban Libraries Council 1993, 1). The American Library Association has had a long-standing policy opposing the charging of fees in publicly supported libraries. This policy (50.3) reads:

> The American Library Association asserts that the charging of fees and levies for information services, including those services utilizing the latest information technology, is discriminatory in publicly supported institutions providing library and information services.
>
> The American Library Association shall seek to make it possible for library and information service agencies which receive their major support from public funds to provide service to all people without additional fees and to utilize the latest technological developments to insure the best access to information, and ALA will actively promote its position on equal access to information (American Library Association 1994, 141).

Given the contrast between these words and the widespread charging of fees in public libraries across the country as of this writing, this policy has been and continues to be the topic of much debate among members of the American Library Association. In fact, the Public Policy for Public Libraries Section of the Public Library Association held open hearings on a proposed position paper on fee-based services at the ALA Midwinter Meeting in February 1995. That draft stated that "beyond locally identified basic services, fees may be charged for: services that provide greater convenience to the customer; an enhanced level of service; services that would otherwise not be available; consumable supplies; service to non-residents" (Shaffer 1994, 333). Both the profession's reaction to this proposed shift in policy and the public's acceptance of public library fees will be interesting to watch and may be bellwethers of our country's shift from believing in equal access to information for all to accepting that people's economic ability—and willingness—to pay for information directly affects the quality and quantity of information available to them.

ALA's position is and has long been that "all information resources that are provided directly or indirectly by the library, regardless of technology, format, or methods of delivery, should be readily, equally and equitably accessible to all library users" (American Library Association 1993). In acknowledging the financial realities facing libraries in today's economic climate, ALA's Council in 1993 affirmed that librarians and governing bodies "should resist the temptation to impose user fees to alleviate financial pressures, at long term cost to institutional integrity and public confidence in libraries" (ALA 1993). ALA policy also includes a statement on library services to the poor that encompasses fifteen policy objectives. The first of these fifteen calls for "promoting the removal of all barriers to library and information services, particularly fees and overdue charges" (American Library Association 1994, 148).

Clearly, the decision to charge fees for information services is not an easy one. It often puts librarians in a catch-22 situation in which they either choose to deprive all users of access to expensive information services or to provide access to those same services for users who are able and willing to pay for it. For librarians who seek to uphold the profession's noblest traditions and principles, the choice can only be to provide ready, equal, and equitable access to information regardless of format. This choice means foregoing fees so that all people can access all information.

THE PUBLIC LIBRARY CHALLENGE

Public libraries are unique institutions in our society; they seek to provide information equity in an inherently unequal information economy. As publicly supported governmental entities, public libraries are very often caught in today's divisive partisan politics. Public library directors must simultaneously cope with tax-reduction rebellions, multiple challenges from the religious right, and the need to remain relevant in the information age with static or shrinking budgets. At the same time they must also tend to the normal business of trying to improve library services and maintain day-to-day operations.

No one contends that this is an easy, or even a manageable task. No one pretends that public librarians have time to go away and reflect on their role in maintaining the library as the arsenal of democracy and think about what that means in an electronic era. It is important, nonetheless, that as public libraries develop and implement policies and procedures that such development and implementation be grounded in sound intellectual freedom philosophies and practices.

Librarians and trustees must work as a team in policy development; the community must perceive that both seek to meet the needs of all the people in the community. Policies are not merely words written on a page and stuck away in a dusty notebook; if everyday practice does not reflect board-approved policy, the chances of a challenge being successful increase greatly. That board-approved policy is based on the Library Bill of Rights and its interpretations, that librarians subscribe to the ALA Code of Ethics, and that all members of the library community uphold First Amendment principles guarantee future generations of users the benefits of a long and noble tradition of public library service.

REFERENCES

American Library Association. "ALA Policy Manual" in *Handbook of Organization 1994/1995*. Chicago: American Library Association, 1994.

American Library Association. "Economic Barriers to Information Access: An Interpretation of the Library Bill of Rights." Chicago: American Library Trustee Association, 1993.

Arney, Mary. *Library Trustees—Who Are They and How Do They Get There?* Chicago: American Library Trustee Association, 1988.

Association of American Publishers, Freedom to Read Committee. "Books and the Young Reader." Washington, DC: Association of American Publishers, n.d.

Krug, Judith F., and Alex P. Allain. "The Trustee and Intellectual Freedom" in Virginia Young. *The Library Trustee: A Practical Guidebook*. 4th ed. Chicago: American Library Association, 1988.

Michigan Library Association, Intellectual Freedom Committee. "Some Words for the Concerned Citizen." Lansing, MI: Michigan Library Association, 1982.

National Center for Education Statistics. *Public Libraries in the United States: 1992*. Washington, DC: U.S. Department of Education, 1994.

Public Library Association. *Statistical Report '94*. Chicago: Public Library Association, 1994.

Seattle Public Library. "Dear Parent or Guardian." Seattle: Seattle Public Library, 1982.

Shaffer, Dallas. "Fee or Free?" *Public Libraries* (November/December 1994).

Urban Libraries Council. "Fees: Survey Results." Evanston, IL: Urban Libraries Council, 1993.

Williams, Lorraine M. *The Library Trustee and the Public Librarian: Partners in Service*. Metuchen, NJ: Scarecrow Press, 1993.

Young, Heatsill, ed. *The ALA Glossary of Library and Information Science*. Chicago: American Library Association, 1983.

4 CONSIDERATIONS SPECIFIC TO SCHOOL LIBRARIES

School libraries must operate within the broader context of both the individual school and the rapidly changing nature of education today. Censorship attempts pertaining to general educational materials and to library materials in particular grow every year. This chapter explores the specific context within which school library media centers exist, the intellectual freedom implications of the mission identified in Information Power *(the current national guidelines for school library media programs), and the legal basis affecting selection of library materials and censorship in school libraries. Tips are presented for working with other parts of the school community, especially parents and administrators.*

The school library media program plays a unique role in promoting intellectual freedom. It serves as a point of voluntary access to information and ideas and as a learning laboratory for students as they acquire critical thinking and problem solving skills needed in a pluralistic society. Although the educational level and program of the school necessarily shapes the resources and services of a school library media program, the principles of the Library Bill of Rights apply equally to all libraries, including school library media programs.

The above quotation is the opening paragraph from the American Library Association's "Access to Resources and Services in the School Library Media Program: An Interpretation of the Library Bill of Rights." This and other interpretations of the Library Bill of Rights can be invaluable to school library media specialists; they are reprinted in Appendix A.

School library media specialists work within a much larger system, which, in many communities, has been under attack from parents and from organized groups most often representing the religious right. Before looking specifically at censorship issues affecting school libraries, we'll consider the educational environment school libraries must function in.

PUBLIC EDUCATION TODAY

The 1980s and 1990s may well be remembered as the bleak years of American education. All over the United States school districts are restructuring and undergoing change. These efforts to improve the quality of education are often hampered by opposition from parents and from community groups who see change and innovation as being in conflict with their religious values.

The responsibility for overall direction of a school district, for supporting educational change, and for dealing with opposition from parent and community groups rests with the district's governing body, the local board of education. Each year communities all over the nation hold elections to choose local school board members. The men and women elected to hold office play an important role in the direction of education in the United States. Boards of education are *the* local policymakers. They are ultimately responsible for the education of students in their school districts, and often find themselves caught in the "culture wars," a clash in values between parents with conservative views of public education and those with more liberal opinions and expectations. The majority of parents want public education to produce responsible, productive citizens. They want young people to be taught to think critically, to learn about and respect the views of those who are different from them, and to be exposed to and appreciate a broad spectrum of ideas.

School board members carry out their responsibilities by hiring (and firing) the superintendent, who is responsible for the day-to-day operation of the school district, by adopting budgets that fund all programs in a school district, and by directing school staff to implement the policies and directions that they set. In terms of libraries and censorship, school boards can be advocates for students by urging administrators to fund library programs adequately and by promulgating strong policies on academic freedom, controversial issues, antidiscrimination, and the selection and reconsideration of educational materials. School boards also serve as the decision makers in the final step of a censorship challenge at the local level, the appeal process.

The religious right political movement has targeted many areas of public school education. These include sexuality education, outcome-based education, self-esteem programs, counseling and drug abuse prevention programs, testing, creationism versus evolution, and multiculturalism. One of the many methods that groups and individuals use to try to protect their children from harm is by attempting to control educational materials used in schools. As an example, the case study chapter, chapter 7, chronicles more than a year of a school district's experience with simultaneous book challenges in several elementary schools, subsequent policy revisions, another book challenge, and a school board election.

Today's public schools are expected to do more for students using less money. Many school board members, superintendents, administrators, teachers, and librarians are finding their environment increasingly challenging as resources shrink, positions are cut from district budgets, and educational materials selected for use in schools are targeted for removal by the same groups objecting to educational change in the public schools. Henry Reichman, in *Censorship and Selection: Issues and Answers for Schools,* states, "Although censors almost invariably claim to be defending American values, educational censorship is harmful precisely because it undermines those very democratic values of tolerance and intellectual freedom our educational system must seek to instill" (Reichman 1993, 3–4).

Every year People for the American Way, an organization devoted to promoting tolerance and protecting constitutional liberties, publishes a survey of censorship and related challenges to public education, *Attacks on the Freedom to Learn.* Some of the trends noted in the 1993–94 report include:

- Attacks overall to curriculum and textbooks continued to rise.
- Challenged material was removed or restricted in 42 percent of censorship attempts, a gain of 8 percent over the previous year's report.
- No area of public education was left unaffected by objectors.
- Religious right political groups initiated 22 percent of all reported incidents.
- The most frequent complaints were about sexual content and objectionable language. The next most frequent category was against material at odds with the objector's religion.
- Reported challenges to anti-gay material continued to rise.
- Teachers and librarians were harassed and fired because of challenges.
- Student newspapers, school plays, and student magazines were frequent targets for objectors.
- Moving library materials to teachers-only, or reserve shelves, or reclassifying material was often used to defuse controversy.

Censorship occurs more frequently than we imagine, and the odds that it will happen in more school districts is increasing. Many censorship incidents are handled internally and are never reported. Others are handled according to school district policy but are never reported either to the American Library Association or People for the American Way.

Given all of the factors, internal and external, that are brought to bear on school libraries, preparation for handling challenges becomes crucial. But just being prepared to "do battle" over a book isn't enough. School librarians, principals, and administrators also need to look at new ways to address the censorship issues. Compromise is not the answer—it just leads to more censorship incidents. When parents attempt to censor materials in school libraries book by book, districts find that these battles are costly in time to librarians, principals, and superintendents. Book battles lower school morale and foster negative relationships between the school and the community. School boards need to find ways to help parents to air their issues by being heard before challenges occur.

Although the public library may be part of a larger municipal government, it appears to stand alone as a great and proud institution in our society. The school library, which is part of a much larger organization, does not enjoy the prominence or the autonomy of the public library. Many of the problems that school librarians are facing with censorship in the 1990s are directly related to the problems facing public education. In a day in which parents challenge every aspect of public education, it is not surprising that library materials are also under siege. Collections are organized to be accessible; any parent can come in and see what's available and check material out. If the librarian is doing his or her job, even school libraries have something to offend everyone.

THE SCHOOL LIBRARY MISSION AND INTELLECTUAL FREEDOM

Information Power: Guidelines for School Library Media Programs states that the "mission of the library media program is to ensure that students and staff are effective users of ideas and information." In carrying out this mission, *Information Power* notes, school librarians face several challenges:

> to provide intellectual and physical access to information and ideas for a diverse population whose needs are changing rapidly
>
> to ensure equity and freedom of access to information and ideas, unimpeded by social, cultural, economic, geographic, or technological constraints
>
> to promote literacy and the enjoyment of reading, viewing, listening for young people at all ages and stages of development
>
> to provide leadership and expertise in the use of information and instructional technologies
>
> and
>
> to participate in networks that enhance access to resources located outside the school (American Association of School Librarians 1988, 3–12).

Although the challenges above speak to five different areas of service to students and teachers, each one, when woven throughout the fabric of a school library media program invites the would-be censor to take a closer look at the library's program.

Many school libraries are not staffed by M.L.S. librarians; some are staffed only by clerks or parent volunteers, and some are not staffed at all. There is much pressure brought to bear on many library staffs to *sanitize* collections—buy nothing that will offend anybody. Many youth librarians are not taking the leadership to provide diverse collections—particularly in school libraries—because of the potential risks involved. We have only to read some of the most vocal youth advocates of our times to learn why this will be detrimental to society in the long run.

In 1979 Dorothy Broderick wrote:

> We cannot protect our youth from the great threats of society, so we must turn to protect them in the only areas in which we have any sense of control at all—we direct our energies at censoring what young people will be allowed to read, hear, and view. Librarians engage in this protectionist philosophy by nonselection of materials and lofty pronouncements about our mission as transmitter of our cultural heritage. Other adults form groups and mobilize to attack materials in schools and libraries, and they are labeled censors. But the only difference between them and *most* librarians is that the range of materials they find offensive is broader than ours, so inadvertently we occasionally buy items that will cause trouble. (There are *some* librarians who conscientiously and systematically buy a wide range of materials reflecting

all available standards of taste and viewpoints, but they are so few as to not warrant consideration here.) (Broderick 1979, 224–25).

Kay Vandergrift, in *Wilson Library Bulletin*, wrote:

As we approach the twenty-first century, library professionals, especially those working with young people, need to take the lead in building collections that are gender-fair and multicultural. We must be willing to take risks in introducing literature of underrepresented peoples and alternative lifestyles into our collection. By excluding such books, we exclude whole groups of young people and make them outcasts of what is perpetuated as the dominant culture (Vandergrift 1993, 26).

Dorothy Broderick wrote her invective against librarians over 15 years ago; Kay Vandergrift's comments are current. Has anything changed in that time? Are school librarians still afraid—or even more afraid—to provide diverse collections? Are we serving the children who come from strong religious backgrounds, particularly the Christian right, with the kinds of materials their parents want them to read? Are we also serving the children of parents of the left, right, and middle? Are we serving children who live in alternative lifestyles, children of gay and lesbian parents? In a recent meeting in the Juneau (Alaska) School District, an elementary school counselor reported that he had documented 14 different types of family structures for the children in that school.

Are our collections diverse? Are they balanced? Do they represent a wide variety of viewpoints? And more importantly, if you work in a school that is nearly homogeneous, does the collection include materials that speak to the diversity of our society and expand the students' horizons?

It is not the libraries in which the librarians systematically avoid buying anything controversial that are vulnerable; it is not the libraries where librarians have bowed to pressures from administrators, boards and teachers to remove "offending" materials that are vulnerable. It is the libraries staffed by librarians who take seriously the challenges put forth in *Information Power* who find themselves increasingly at risk, and they fight censorship battles often on two fronts—with those in the community who seek to challenge material using the reconsideration process and with their colleagues in the school district who would also seek to censor.

School librarians must confront the traditional inclination of adults to try to set limits for children daily. Today's emphasis on

preparing children and young adults for a diverse work force adds
to the close scrutiny of today's educators. Just as educational goals
and programs geared to the lowest common denominator irrepa-
rably harm the curriculum, so, too, does sanitizing the library's
collection.

THE LEGAL BASIS FOR SCHOOL CENSORSHIP

Tinker v. *Des Moines Independent School District* was not a case
about school libraries nor did it involve censorship of library
materials. It was, however, a landmark Supreme Court case quoted
widely in the library literature because the Court held that neither "students [n]or teachers shed their constitutional rights to
freedom of speech or expression at the school house gate." Censorship has always existed in schools, but it wasn't until 1982
that the U.S. Supreme Court ruled on a case that directly involved
school censorship, *Board of Education, Island Trees Union Free
School District* v. *Pico*, often referred to as the *Pico* case or the
Island Trees case. This legal case, which often guides school districts in responding to today's censorship challenges, reached the
Supreme Court in 1982, six years after the original censorship
incident. The Island Trees Board of Education removed nine books
from the school library's shelves. Several students, including Steven
Pico, sued to have them returned. The *Pico* case was a class action suit, representing all students in the school district. They felt
that the school board violated their constitutional rights and the
academic freedom rights of librarians and teachers. It was also
argued that the school board's reason for banning the books was
political and not educational.

The Supreme Court justices ruled that school boards do not
have unfettered authority to select library books and that students' First Amendment rights are violated when books are removed arbitrarily. The Court also ruled against motivated book
removals. Justice Brennan in the majority decision wrote, "We
hold that local school boards may not remove books from school
library shelves simply because they dislike the ideas contained in
these books and seek by their removal to prescribe what shall be
orthodox in politics, nationalism, religion or other matters of
opinion."

Steven Pico, in a speech to the Missouri Association of School

Librarians in 1989, stated, "The Court ruled 5–4 in my behalf. The decision was not a sweeping condemnation of book banning which had been hoped for. We won by the skin of our teeth. But do not underestimate the importance of this decision" (Pico 1990, 86).

If you have never read a Supreme Court case with its majority and minority opinions, the *Pico* case is a good place for school librarians to start. Knowing and being able to explain this landmark Supreme Court decision can be of invaluable help to librarians seeking to protect their students' right to read.

While *Pico* was a landmark case, it was not at all clear-cut. Four of the nine justices did not see that this case involved First Amendment issues. As Pico went on to say to the Missouri librarians, "The Supreme Court agreed to hear the Pico case in the first place because these four dissenting justices [Rehnquist, O'Connor, Powell, and Burger] believed that they could convince a fifth justice to side with them and make book banning constitutionally permissible . . . but the fifth vote they were counting on never materialized. . . . Legally speaking, the Pico case is a very fragile victory, but I assure you it will stand for some time, perhaps decades."

An excellent overview of notable First Amendment court cases is in the *Banned Books Resource Guide*, available from the Office for Intellectual Freedom, American Library Association.

WHO IS ATTEMPTING TO CENSOR?

Many materials challenges in school libraries come from individual parents, but librarians should be prepared to deal with challenges from two less obvious sources: school personnel and organized groups.

SCHOOL PERSONNEL

Unlike the public library, where very few censorship challenges are internally instigated, in school districts many of the attempts to restrict access to information come not from religious groups or parents but from school district employees. School boards, teachers, superintendents, or principals will request that material be restricted or removed from library collection. Their efforts are often successful because of their position within the school district, and it is primarily because of their positions within the school that they seek to have materials restricted or removed without going through the formal reconsideration process described in chapter 6.

This is the point where librarians must examine their values and come to a decision. Some librarians remove questioned items immediately. Others have more trouble and would like to say "no" but often end up saying "yes" because of possible consequences. The professionally responsible thing to do is to ask the colleague, boss, or staff member to fill out the reconsideration form. ALA's Office for Intellectual Freedom reported that the majority of challenges in 1994 were from parents (American Library Association, Office for Intellectual Freedom 1995). It is important that the school library media specialist require that *all* challenges be put in writing, not just those of parents.

ORGANIZED GROUPS

There are some groups today that have formed for the sole purpose of giving parents "increased legal muscle when it comes to directing their children's education." One of these new groups is called Of the People. It has introduced a Parental Rights Amendment in several states that reads, "The rights of parents to direct the upbringing and education of their children shall not be infringed" (School Library Journal, 10–11). Finding ways to work with conservative parents and the groups they belong to is going to be more and more important as collections come under attack.

PARENTS

Many parents naturally expect the school, including the school librarian, to guide their children's reading carefully. Inevitably though, conflicts arise between what librarians may select and put on library shelves and what parents may wish their children to read.

Parents, in the course of censorship incidents, often refer to the term *in loco parentis*. A legal term, *in loco parentis* means in place of a parent; charged with a parent's rights, duties, and responsibilities. While teachers act *in loco parentis* for students during the school day, one can assert that school librarians, in fact, do not act *in loco parentis*, except for matters of health and safety. Judith Krug, director of ALA's Office for Intellectual Freedom, stated in an interview,

> Libraries not only provide ideas and information important to young people in the school setting but they also provide choice. School libraries are governed by the curriculum which is set by regulations from the state, by the school board, by

teachers and by the community. Schools fulfill a need for all kids within a given set of parameters. School librarians serve the interests of the public in educating all the children who go to school in a school district. They are not responsible for every requirement set down by every parent in that community. Not all children march to the same drummer. All children do not believe the same things. All children do not practice the same religion. That is why there are policies and procedures which govern the selection process, and which provide for a broad array of ideas and information from which the students can choose (Krug, 1995).

Parents, and only parents, can restrict what their child can read. Librarians do not have the responsibility to restrict materials for individual children. In fact, librarians should never agree to restrict access for individual children. Libraries are about access, not about restricting materials. Parents often comment that with library automation, the task is easy—"Just set up the automated system so that when my son or daughter comes to the desk with a book I don't want him or her to read, you will insure that *my* child does not check out the book." In working with automated systems, talking to vendors at conferences, and visiting public and school libraries, the authors have never found a library vendor who markets a module for an automated system designed to restrict access.

A sentence that states, "The library accepts no responsibility for enforcing what a parent may not want a child to see, read, or view while in the library" should be part of every library's policy or procedures. "Free Access to Libraries for Minors: An Interpretation of the Library Bill of Rights" is very clear on this point:

> Librarians and governing bodies should maintain that parents—and only parents—have the right and responsibility to restrict the access of their children—and only their children—to library resources. Parents or legal guardians who do not want their children to have access to certain library services, materials or facilities, should so advise their children. Librarians and governing bodies cannot assume the role of parents or the functions of parental authority in the private relationship between parent and child.

Parents do have a right to control access—but only for their own children. While the librarian can help parents and children select materials, libraries, even school libraries, have tradition-

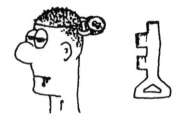

Censorship is not the key to unlocking young minds

ally maintained neutral roles. The library's job does not include assisting parents in enforcing their own family rules and values. Perhaps the best example in the United States of parents who live what they preach is the Jehovah's Witnesses. There are certain types of materials they do not want their children to read, children are so instructed by their parents, and parents acknowledge that it is the responsibility of the child to stick within the boundaries set by the parent.

WORKING WITH PARENTS AND BOARD MEMBERS

Librarians work with children, young adults, and teachers in the course of their daily work. Working with parents is also an important part of the job of promoting school libraries and making parents aware of the library's mission.

School library media specialists can make their job easier and gain supporters by making time to talk to parents and invite them into the library. In meeting with parents it is important to listen to what they are telling you. Ask questions: Does your collection meet the reading and informational needs of their child? You can also talk about the parents' right to control what their child reads.

If parents have concerns about their children's access to materials in the library, encourage them to guide and monitor what their children read. Do not agree to remove the books from circulation or the collection, but explain the reconsideration process and why it's there.

Parents are your allies, not enemies. Try to be flexible and involve parents in the activities of the library. Start a friends of school libraries group in your school or community. Ask parents to make suggestions and make a patron suggestion form a part of every newsletter. Use parent volunteers for a specific purpose, such as story reading, and invite parents from different cultural backgrounds to give programs in the library. Train parents in the use of library computers; invite them in to try out new technology, such as CD-ROM products and the Internet. Give parents a library card!

When a concerned parent wants to speak with you and the principal, take this opportunity to educate both of them. The difference between a concerned parent and one who wishes to censor is that the concerned parent is interested only in talking about materials for his or her child. You know you have a problem when the "concerned parent" is interested in protecting all the children in a community and claims to be speaking for all the parents in the community.

Whether they work in a school district with one librarian or hundreds, politically savvy librarians will get to know their school board members. There are several ways to do this:

- Encourage good people you know in the community to run for the board and support them.
- Volunteer to serve on your teachers' association political action committee, if you have one.
- Take an active part in the League of Women Voters.
- Attend school board meetings.

Make sure that at least one school librarian is in attendance at every school board meeting during the year. Informal chats occur at the beginning of the meetings where you can introduce yourself, ensure that your presence has been noted, and demonstrate that you are interested in what the school board does. Then, when items come up that deal with school libraries, librarians are "faces," not just names whose issues are to be dealt with.

Libraries, particularly in schools, are only one part of a much larger organization. Complications often arise from being the only voice for intellectual freedom in the school building. There is a public perception that restriction is more appropriate in a school, where attendance is mandatory, than in a public library. In schools there is also the greater likelihood of pressure from your administrator. These factors make censorship of a given title more likely in a school than in a public library. All who care about schools, youth, and libraries must be vigilant in keeping access to a wide variety of materials a top priority.

REFERENCES

American Association of School Librarians and Association for Educational Communications and Technology. *Information Power: Guidelines for School Library Media Programs.* Chicago: American Library Association; Washington D.C.: Association for Educational Communications and Technology, 1988.

American Library Association. "Access to Resources and Services in the School Library Media Program: An Interpretation of the Library Bill of Rights." Chicago: American Library Association, 1990.

American Library Association. Office for Intellectual Freedom. "OIF Censorship Database 1994." Chicago: American Library Association, 1995.

Attacks on the Freedom to Learn: 1993–1994 Report. Washington, DC: People for the American Way, 1994.

Board of Education, Island Trees Union Free School District No. 26 v. *Pico,* 457 U.S. 873, 102 S.Ct. 2799, 73 L.Ed.2nd 435 (1982).

Broderick, Dorothy M. "Censorship: A Family Affair?" *Top of the News.* (Spring 1979).

Duby, Deanna, and Mark Sedway. "Protecting the Freedom to Learn" in *How to Win: A Practical Guide for Defeating the Radical Right in Your Community.* Comp. by Radical Right Task Force, National Jewish Democratic Council. Washington, DC: The Council, 1994.

"Free Access to Libraries for Minors: An Interpretation of the Library Bill of Rights." Chicago: American Library Association, 1991.

Krug, Judith. Telephone Interview, April 18, 1995.

"Parents' Rights Lobby Pushes for More Classroom Control." *School Library Journal* (October 1994).

Pico, Steven. "An Introduction to Censorship." *School Library Media Quarterly* (Winter, 1990).

"Public Education Advocacy: 4—Targets: Important Educational Policies Influenced by the Religious Right Political Movement" in *An Activist's Guide to Protecting the Freedom to Learn.* Washington, DC: People for the American Way, 1994.

Reichman, Henry. *Censorship and Selection: Issues and Answers for Schools.* Rev. ed. Chicago: American Library Association; Arlington, VA: American Association of School Administrators, 1993.

Tinker v. *Des Moines School District*, 393 U.S. 503, 89 S.Ct 736, 21 L.Ed.2nd.731 (1969).

Vandergrift, Kay. "A Feminist Research Agenda in Youth Literature." *Wilson Library Bulletin* (October 1993).

5 PROTECTING INTELLECTUAL FREEDOM ON THE INFORMATION SUPERHIGHWAY

Basic questions regarding providing access to Internet resources challenge every librarian who first seeks to make the Net available in his or her library. This chapter defines what providing access means, discusses policies and procedures regarding Internet access in libraries, analyzes four issues that providing access commonly presents for libraries, discusses technical mechanisms some libraries use to facilitate access to recommended Net resources without infringing upon intellectual freedom, notes technology that is not recommended because it violates the Library Bill of Rights, and points readers to resources on the Net that can provide further information.

No other phenomenon has so totally altered the whole landscape of American culture as quickly as the Internet. Just ten years ago, the idea of subnotebook computers weighing less than four pounds communicating with mainframe computers thousands of miles away via cellular modems would have been thought by all but the most avid technoenthusiast to be a pipe dream; today, it is a reality.

In addition to utilizing the greatly expanded information sources the Internet makes available, librarians have an obligation to provide access to the Internet in or through their institutions so that our society does not become divided into two new classes: the information haves and the information have-nots. In an issue of *Time* magazine devoted to cyberspace, Suneel Ratan pointed out that in 1995, people who could use a computer already earned 15 percent more than those who could not. With the growing importance of the Internet, Ratan said, "Access to the information highway may determine the basic ability to function in a democratic culture" (Ratan 1995, 25). Since Internet access for most people who do not work in universities, large corporations, or government organizations requires personal ownership of computer equipment and payment of fees for online services, many people are barred from equal participation in our society unless they have access through local libraries. Such services continue the role libraries have traditionally played of ensuring free and open access to information of all kinds.

Librarians are already influencing America's future by making technology available to students. A 1995 survey by the American Electronics Association's National Information Infrastructure Task Force found that while only 20 percent of teachers surveyed had an Internet account, more than half of school librarians surveyed did ("High-Tech . . . " 1995, A19). This incredible variance means that school library media specialists are more than twice as likely as classroom teachers to be able to expose students to the possibilities of electronic communication, Internet resources, and scholarly newsgroups.

INTERNET ACCESS IN LIBRARIES

The incredible power of the Internet, the network of networks, has quite literally transformed the way we communicate, the way we transfer information, what we know, and when we know it. Virtual communities have sprung up. Whole new ways of affecting the political process and public opinion are used every day that were not even thought of five years ago. This incredible power reaches its maximum potential through libraries because they can ensure access for all people in the community regardless of their economic status. People can use Internet connections provided both through and at libraries to communicate with governmental representatives and officials, participate in electronic discussions (just as they might participate in a discussion held in a library meeting room), access online resources, get information on national and international affairs as they happen, and expand their horizons beyond limitation. Public library patrons in the smallest and most remote community and students in the poorest school library can have access to satellite photos, see and talk with scientists in Antarctica, exchange e-mail with Chinese revolutionaries, take a tour of the White House, download the latest Senate bill, and view images seen through telescopes on other continents. The same resource that brings all these wonderful possibilities into our businesses, homes, classrooms, and libraries also brings recipes for making marijuana brownies, pictures of sexual acts that would challenge the most accomplished contortionist, bawdy limericks, erotic stories, discussion groups devoted to pedophilia and bondage, and instructions for accessing even more sexual content. The satellite photos and the pictures of sexual acts are equally detailed; access to both is easy and free.

Because providing access to the Internet brings with it such a wide range of resources, choosing to bring the Internet into your library is like buying an anthology of 33 short stories: you either buy it or you don't, and if you buy it, you make all of it accessible to all your patrons. You don't go through the stories and excise the two that don't meet your selection criteria (this would be expurgation, a violation of the Library Bill of Rights); you don't put a label on it reading, "Warning: Two of these short stories are smutty" (labeling, another violation); you don't put it behind the reference desk and ask for picture ID proving users are 18 or over before they can have it (restricted access, again, a violation); and, if you found 2 of the 33 short stories to be personally offensive, you don't refuse to buy it in the first place (that would be censorship, not selection). Likewise, when librarians choose to bring the Internet into their library, they bring the whole thing: the good, the breathtakingly amazing, the bad, and the very ugly.

However, choosing to provide Internet access in libraries is different than buying a printed anthology of short stories for a number of reasons: (1) if a library is financially able to provide Internet access, not doing so would be deliberately choosing to deprive patrons of access to a world of information and communication; (2) in a few years, any library not providing access to information via the Internet will be bypassed by patrons needing current information—in essence, the library would be making a choice to become an irrelevant dinosaur; (3) much information in the future will be published only electronically; and (4) providing access to the Internet isn't an act of "buying," but rather one of facilitating access.

The challenge librarians must face in administering access to the Internet is two-fold. First, they must appropriate the necessary funds, technology, infrastructure, and expertise to make this new world accessible to themselves and their patrons. Second, they must deal with the fallout that results when people and their children can suddenly read, view, and listen to almost anything they choose. Issues related to technology, infrastructure, and technological expertise are beyond the domain of this book. Readers seeking this kind of information are referred to Alan Benson's *The Complete Internet Companion for Librarians* (Neal-Schuman, 1995) and other sources available in the library literature. Once the library has acquired the needed hardware, software, and infrastructure, any decision to charge fees has definite intellectual freedom implications; for a discussion of these issues refer to the section on fees in chapter 3 of this book.

Libraries across the country are already doing extraordinary things with the Internet. For example, homeless people are accessing the Internet at the Seattle Public Library, the State Library of Maryland has coordinated statewide Internet access through public libraries (including making state and local government information available through a gopher), and students at all grade levels are accessing heretofore unknown resources through their school libraries. But choosing and making these resources available requires careful planning.

POLICIES AND PROCEDURES FOR INTERNET ACCESS IN LIBRARIES

Libraries can choose to provide Internet access for patrons at the library (onsite) and/or for patrons through the library in their homes and businesses. Whichever choice the library makes, the traditional values that have governed library policies and procedures need to be followed as libraries begin to develop policies and procedures for administering Internet access. ALA has developed one document that will be especially helpful to librarians seeking guidance in developing such policies, the American Library Association "Guidelines for the Development and Implementation of Policies, Regulations and Procedures Affecting Access to Library Materials, Services and Facilities" (reprinted in Appendix A). As this book was going to press, ALA was finalizing a new interpretation of the Library Bill of Rights dealing with access to electronic information, services, and networks. This interpretation is expected to be available in early 1996.

Several key issues about providing access to Internet resources are often bones of contention between librarians and administrators (in schools or in county or municipal government), between librarians and parents, between librarians and concerned citizens, and among librarians themselves. The issues include:

1. Because there is so much explicitly controversial material on the Internet, libraries that provide Internet access are often under pressure to deny or limit access to certain areas of cyberspace.
2. Librarians may discover that some material accessed elec-

tronically in their libraries may not meet their selection criteria or collection development policy or may be inappropriate for the user community.

3. Librarians may discover that some material accessed electronically is inaccurate or misleading.

4. Librarians may discover that as the popularity and usefulness of the Internet grows, demands for access to it bring increased associated costs that some administrators feel they should recover by charging users.

While these issues appear to be overwhelmingly formidable at first glance, developing policies and procedures for addressing them really only requires applying the profession's traditional tenets and the library's existing policies to a new medium. For example, here are some key concepts that should be used in responding to each of the four issues listed above.

1. Just as libraries do not deny or abridge access to books, videos, software, etc., they should not restrict access to electronic information and resources. Parents who are concerned about what their children might access on the Internet should provide guidance to their own children as they use the Internet just as they should when they select books to check out and bring home.

2. Internet access immeasurably extends the library's ability to provide access to information, resources, experts, and electronic discussions relating to the interests of all community members. Librarians must support access to all materials on all subjects for all users. This parallels the arguments supporting diversity in collection development.

3. Libraries have never certified or warranted that any information in any book is accurate or authentic. Just as we do not attempt to check the population figures given in any almanac, the historical accuracy of accounts of the early Christian crusades, or the facts cited in a table listing the calorie content of every candy bar on the market, we do not vouch for the accuracy of information retrieved electronically. Likewise, we do not purport to vouch for or agree with the viewpoints taken in electronic newsgroups any more than we vouch for or agree with editorials in the *New Republic* or the *New York Times*.

4. Once the library decides to provide access to the Internet or any electronic resource, it must provide equitable ac-

cess. This means *free* access. If there is a limited budget, the American Library Association's draft interpretation of the Library Bill of Rights "Access to Electronic Information, Services, and Networks" suggests rationing service as a means of maintaining equity.

Those on the forefront of the cyberwars in libraryland have found out that librarians are already encountering problems. Bruce Flanders, director of technology for the Kansas State Library, talked to school librarians about providing Internet access. He found that "many school librarians are so convinced that 99 percent of the resources on the net are essential that they are willing to risk catching heat from an angry parent or active special interest group" (Flanders 1994, 32–33).

These types of access issues don't stop at school libraries, however. Martin Rimm, a research associate at Carnegie-Mellon University, used university computers to collect 917,000 sexual pictures ranging from simple nudity to bestiality and determined that these pictures had been downloaded 6.4 million times. Since children as young as elementary school age use the university's computer links, Rimm and Edward Steinberg, vice provost for education, felt that the school could be charged with distributing pornography to minors. There was a backlash of protests from students, the faculty senate, and the ACLU when the university decided to cut off access to some Internet sites. Student Council President Declan McCullagh called the ban "the equivalent of closing down a wing of the library," a very apt analogy ("Censorship . . . " 1995, 1).

To facilitate access to particularly valuable parts of the Internet, some libraries have begun designing their own gophers (menus that automatically access Internet sites that users choose) and World Wide Web pages (graphical interfaces to a variety of Net resources). While these mechanisms make accessing chosen information quick and easy as well as perform a reader guidance role, they in no means deny or restrict users from accessing other parts of cyberspace. Because they both perform a service and don't restrict user access, they are a beneficial tool for libraries to use. For excellent examples of such an interface, readers are referred to Indiana University-Purdue University at Indianapolis (IUPUI) Library's IUPUI University Library Information System (http://www-lib.iupui.edu/images/home.gif) and to the Berkeley (California) Public Library's home page (http://www.ci.berkeley.ca.us/bpl).

Creating such technological tools upholds intellectual freedom principles because librarians select resources to which the library facilitates access; it's a positive decision. Technologies that effectively censor the Net are also available, and their use clearly violates intellectual freedom. One example of such a product is *SurfWatch*, which according to promotional literature distributed in May 1995 "comes ready to block hundreds of sites containing material we do not want our children to see." Progressive Networks, Microsoft, and Netscape announced plans in the summer of 1995 to form the Information Highway Parental Empowerment Group to allow parents and others to lock out sites with sexual content. Libraries that adopt such draconian measures clearly abdicate their selection responsibilities to a commercial product as well as violate the second sentence of Article II of the Library Bill of Rights ("Materials should not be proscribed or removed because of partisan or doctrinal disapproval").

Another tactic libraries use when providing Internet access for minors is parental education. Libraries can do this by informing parents that their children may access controversial or offensive materials and that it is the parents' responsibility to provide guidance in this area. Such notification follows the tradition of not having libraries act *in loco parentis* and at the same time communicates to parents information about a new technology that they may be unfamiliar with. The Juneau (Alaska) School District, for instance, has developed a Code of Conduct that accompanies such parental notification. The Code of Conduct and a parental notification letter for Juneau-Douglas High School are reprinted in Figures 5–1 and 5–2.

This tactic is less desirable than simply making Internet resources available on the same basis as all other library resources. However, it is certainly preferable to restricted or monitored Internet access.

STRENGTHENING INTELLECTUAL FREEDOM ELECTRONICALLY

Not surprisingly, librarians are already not only navigating the information superhighway and helping others to access electronic information, but we are also leading the way in developing the global village.

Students at the University of Michigan's School of Information and Library Science recently developed the Internet Public Library. This World Wide Web site's mission is "to provide services and

---

FIGURE 5-1   Juneau School District's Network Code of Conduct

Code of Conduct for Network Services

Definitions

Network Services refers to the services provided on the local area network within the school, and the wide area network throughout the district including Internet connectivity available from the desktops of computers on the network.

These services include:
- Access to word processing, spreadsheet, database, paint and draw, multimedia, presentation and other tools available on the network.
- Access to the school library catalog system at the Capital City Libraries.
- Access to shared files and publications available on the wide area network.
- Access to Internet for information gathering, communications and publishing.

Network Users refers to students, staff and others given access to the school network services.

Rights

Users have the right to:
- use available technology including network services in their daily learning.
- examine a broad range of opinions and ideas in the educational process including the right to locate, use and exchange information and ideas using network services.
- communicate with other individuals including those accessible using network services.

Responsibilities

Users have the responsibility to:
- use school district hardware and software competently and respectfully.
- learn to use the network services needed.
- monitor personal file space.
- follow all state and federal statutes regarding copyright and technology use.
- maintain and respect the privacy of the user accounts and activities of all.
- follow the established guidelines for computer etiquette.
- report any violation to network services personnel.

Unacceptable Uses

Users may not:
- damage or disrupt equipment or system performance.
- corrupt the data of another user.
- waste resources such as paper, time or access for others.
- participate in malicious hacking such as gaining unauthorized access to any resources.
- invade the privacy of others by activities such as eavesdropping or reading someone else's mail or files.
- use or publish information about an account owned by another user.
- use profanity, obscenity or other language which may be offensive to another user.
- post anonymous messages.
- use the network services for any illegal activity such as violation of copyright, plagiarism, or other contractual use agreements.
- allow obscene, disruptive or inappropriate materials to enter the school network.

FIGURE 5-2   Parental Permission Notification Form for Juneau-Douglas High School

August 1995

Dear Parents,

In October of 1993, the Juneau voters passed a technology bond issue which provided for the construction of a district-wide computer network, the automation of library circulation systems in each school, and the purchase of new computers. The Juneau School District now is able to offer vast technology resources including those available on the Internet through the networked computers at each school in the district.

The Internet is an international network of networks and is commonly known as the "information superhighway." Through the Juneau School District Network (JSDNet), your student will have access to the Internet, which includes hundreds of databases, libraries, and resources from all over the world. Additionally, the Internet is a new publishing environment allowing students an audience for their work of potentially millions of users throughout the world. However, because it is diverse, it is also possible that your student may run across areas of adult content and some material you might find objectionable. While we don't encourage access to such material, it is not possible for us to block access to it.

Part of our responsibility in preparing students for the 21st century is to provide them with the tools they will be using as adults. We believe that use of this global information network is one of those tools. With this educational opportunity comes responsibility. We accept responsibility for teaching your students about his/her role as a "network citizen" and the code of conduct involved with use of the Internet. And, we are asking that you have done so by signing and returning the bottom portion of this paper. Except for electronic mail, students do not need a password to use the Internet. Parents or legal guardians who do not want their children to have access to the Internet should so advise their children.

Thank you for helping us provide responsible computer network and Internet use for your student. Together we need to maintain the integrity of this innovative educational resource.

Sincerely,

Ron Gleason, Principal

I/We have reviewed the JSDNet Code of Conduct with our student. I/We agree to support the school and our student in upholding the regulations imposed on the use of the school network.

_____   _____
Parent Signature   Student Signature

Date:

information which enhance the value of the Internet to its ever-expanding and varied community of users; work to broaden, diversify, and educate that community; [and] communicate its creators' vision of the unique role of library culture and traditions on the Internet" (Internet Public Library 1995a). One of the many marvelous aspects of this site is that it transforms traditional library statements and commitments into language and formats appropriate for today's electronic arena.

For example, the Internet Public Library's Materials Reconsideration Policy includes this statement: "Users who wish staff of the Library to reconsider either (a) pointers to materials **outside** the Library'[s] original materials or (b) materials created by members of the Library should email requests to **ipl@umich.edu** and they will be forwarded to the appropriate division. Division coordinators will respond via email to such requests. Appeals are directed to the Director" (Internet Public Library 1995b). Readers are referred to this wonderfully original site (http://www.ipl.sils.umich.edu/) for policy models (such as those cited here and other useful statements like the site's Youth Division Selection Policy) and for ideas about arranging your own library's Web site.

Other resources available to help libraries protect the right to read, view, and listen to Internet resources are acceptable use policies for K–12 schools such as those available through the ERIC Clearinghouse (gopher://ericir.syr.edu/:70/11/Guides), from Rice University (gopher://riceinfo.rice.edu: 8002/7? acceptable K12), and from the California Department of Education (gopher://goldmine.cde.ca.gov: 70/11/C_D_E_Info/Technology/Acceptable_Use), which contains sample policies and forms.

A virtual source of information about First Amendment issues (including those regarding the Internet) is the newly developed First Amendment Cyber-Tribune developed by Charles Levensosky. This site can be accessed at http://W3.trib.com/FACT/. ALA's Office for Intellectual Freedom has a listserv through which librarians can support each other and disseminate information. To subscribe, send the message SUBSCRIBE ALAOIF YOURNAME to listserv@uicvm.uic.edu.

Perhaps the most exciting development in using the Internet to protect intellectual freedom is the World Wide Web home page, which was instigated in 1995 by Karen G. Schneider. This unique site, Karen's Kitchen: The Freedom Pages, contains an amazing amount of helpful information such as sample library policies. The page is also a model of Web page organization. The address is http://www.intoc.com/~legs/freedom/.

In summary, perhaps the most important point to be made about administering Internet access through libraries is that such administration should begin with the same core beliefs and principles that guide all library policies and procedures. Libraries exist primarily to facilitate connections between people and information. In doing so, creating access is always better than creating roadblocks.

REFERENCES

American Library Association. "Access to Electronic Information, Services, and Networks: An Interpretation of the Library Bill of Rights." Draft. Chicago: American Library Association, 1995.

"Censorship on the Internet." *Newsletter on Intellectual Freedom* 45:2 (March 1995), 1.

Flanders, Bruce. "A Delicate Balance." *School Library Journal* (October 1994), 32–33.

"High-Tech Resides in High School Libraries." *Chronicle of Higher Education* (March 31, 1995), A19.

The Internet Public Library. "Mission Statement and Goals." http://www.ipl.sils.umich.edu/. March 20, 1995.

The Internet Public Library. "Materials Reconsideration Policy." http://www.ipl.sils.umich.edu/. March 16, 1995.

Ratan, Suneel. "A New Divide between Haves and Have-Nots?" *Time* 145:12 (Special Issue, Spring 1995), 25.

6 THE RECONSIDERATION PROCESS

While the filing of a "request for reconsideration" is often the most feared event in the whole intellectual freedom arena, reconsideration informally occurs almost every day in almost every library. This chapter looks at a sample reconsideration policy, outlines the five parts that good reconsideration policies or procedures should have, identifies the six basic responsibilities of a reconsideration committee, and presents tips for dealing with a public hearing should there be one. The chapter emphasizes the importance of board-approved policies and ways librarians can prevent formal challenges through listening to and educating patrons about the library's role in serving the whole community.

Just as librarians select books and other items as a part of their professional responsibilities, they also reconsider materials that are a part of existing collections. In fact, some books are reconsidered before they even get on the shelf. For librarians who order primarily from reviews, occasionally what arrives is a surprise. For instance, a high school librarian orders a book that, it turns out, is better suited to a middle school or junior high. He or she might then send it to another library. In another common situation, a librarian comes across a book on the shelf that clearly is out of date, with a later edition in the collection. The solution is to remove the out-of-date book. Or a librarian may ask for a report from the automated system for books in the 500s that haven't been checked out for five years, and then spend some time weeding. Whether you send a book to another library before you put it on the shelf, come across an out-of-date volume accidentally, or systematically weed your collection you are reconsidering the usefulness of items in your collection.

Librarians reconsider materials in accordance with their selection policy. Patrons may also ask for reconsideration of library materials as a First Amendment right, since the First Amendment speaks to petitioning the government for redress of grievances as well as freedom of speech. It is "redress of grievances" that gives any community member the right to question or challenge material in the library collection. In a library setting this process is called *reconsideration*.

The reconsideration process can be viewed as a continuum. Every interaction librarians have with patrons about "problem" materials will fall somewhere along the line. Reconsideration of an item in the library's collection may take as little time as sitting down and having a discussion with a parent, an interested user, or a group of users or it may be a long process that takes months to resolve and consumes a community in heated controversy. It may not end until the U.S. Supreme Court issues a decision. Whatever situation you find yourself in, remember that a person questioning the library collection is exercising his or her right to participate in a democracy. Censorship incidents are never just about the item in question. Incidents are often about clashes in values and about the First Amendment and the freedoms it provides. The material is often a symbol of such differences in values and beliefs.

Good policy and procedures play an important role in censorship incidents—and it is just "good business" to have them. Every library should have a board-approved reconsideration policy, and there should be procedures to be followed when a reconsideration request is made. School librarians, in particular, also need to ensure that administrators and teachers are familiar with the district's policies and procedures, understand that they pertain to all persons (both inside and outside the organization), and realize that librarians are prepared to defend the process. One of the fastest ways to get in legal trouble is by not following your own procedures.

The chances are that in every library someone will eventually question a librarian's selection decision. Before looking at what should be in a reconsideration policy, let's take a quick look at what most complaints are about. It is no surprise to anybody who follows censorship incidents and who looks at the American Library Association's Office for Intellectual Freedom *Banned Books Week Resource Guide* each year that challenges have risen over the past five years. Statistics for 1994 kept by the ALA Office for Intellectual Freedom (American Library Association 1995) show that the top categories of materials that are targets for censorship are:

1. Homosexuality (including homosexual lifestyles)
2. Occult/satan (including witchcraft, the supernatural, Halloween)
3. Sexuality (including sex education, nudity, sex education, materials with explicit sex)
4. Materials with offensive language

THE RECONSIDERATION POLICY

A reconsideration policy outlines the process that a library or school district follows when asked to reconsider material. There are many models and sample policies in library literature. Some are very general and others are incredibly specific. It is important that your library have a policy that will serve the needs of the school district or library, that this policy is followed, and that it is not changed during a censorship incident. Plan on evaluating your policy after any censorship incident where it is used.

One of the most important points that should be included in the policy and procedures is that the challenged material should remain in circulation until the end of the challenge. Removing the material during the challenge defeats the process and denies users access to the material.

Challenges might be made by an individual, group, parent, legislator, teacher, student, board member, school administrator, or school superintendent, and they include a variety of requested actions—restriction, reclassification, or removal.

A short reconsideration policy for a public library might look like this:

> Citizens wishing reconsideration of library materials should complete the "Request for Reconsideration of Library Materials" form. This form is available at all branches of the library or may be obtained through the Director's Office. Such requests concerning adult material are directed to the Adult Services Coordinator, and requests concerning juvenile materials are directed to the Children's Coordinator. If published reviews of the material in question are available, they will be sent along with the Reconsideration Request form to the Library Director.
>
> The Director will ask three staff members to evaluate the material in light of the patron's request using published reviews and the above criteria [in the collection development policy]. Evaluators will submit their recommendations to the Director, who will make a decision concerning the material. The process will result in maintaining the current status, a change in location or reading level, or removal.
>
> The Director will notify the patron originating the Reconsideration Request of the decision. If the individual is not satisfied with the action taken, he/she may appeal to the Library Board (Schexnaydre 1984, 78).

The above policy is very brief. The basics are included but it provides a few details. Do not write something that is so bogged down in detail that the timelines in them may be difficult to meet: in five days this will happen, another five days for the next part to happen. Sometimes it takes more than five days to find a copy of the book, especially if the complainant has the only copy and isn't returning it. Seek a balance between being too general and too specific. Always be sure that new policies/procedures are in the same format as current policies and that the needs of your library or school district are met.

Reconsideration policies/procedures have five basic parts:

1. An introduction describing the process and often outlining informal methods of dealing with questions about materials;
2. A reconsideration form to be given to patrons who wish to fill it out;
3. A design for a committee or group to reconsider material after a formal challenge has been filed;
4. A designated person, often the library director or superintendent, who has the authority to accept or reject the committee's decision; and
5. An appeal process.

Somewhere in the process it may be necessary to hold public hearings. This is most often done during the appeal process, although a committee may need or want to hold hearings as it is doing its work. Whether it is one person, or a group, or 40 people who all fill out the same form for one book, they have one objective—to be heard and to ensure that their concerns are taken seriously.

The informal process may or may not be spelled out in the procedures. It is just plain common sense to sit down informally and talk with a person who expresses a concern about something in the library's collection. Imagine what would happen if every time a parent expressed a concern about a book, a librarian shoved a reconsideration form at him or her and said, "Fine, fill this out and then come back. We'll talk then." June Pinnell-Stephens, chair of Alaska Library Association's Intellectual Freedom Committee since 1984 and a veteran at dealing with challenges, reports that from her personal observation, of every 100 people who come into the library with a concern about a title, 90 leave after such a conversation and are satisfied. Ten take the reconsideration form. Of the ten, only one actually fills it out and turns it in.

Nothing about this process should be secret. When patrons come in to talk, they are more likely to go away satisfied if you share the library's mission, selection policy, and reconsideration process with them and listen to their concerns. If they are not satisfied, they will go away with a reconsideration form and copies of all of your library's policies and procedures pertaining to intellectual freedom. If a patron returns with the form filled out, remember that you have set the stage for the process to be fair and open. Patrons who initiate the challenge are exercising their democratic rights.

Don't get scared or intimidated into removing library material when a hostile patron complains. The same is true if your boss comes to you with a concern about a book. The librarian who attempts to resolve the situation by ignoring the process and hopes the problem "will just go away" is being a "silent censor." Frances Beck McDonald in her book *Censorship and Intellectual Freedom: A Survey of School Librarians' Attitudes and Moral Reasoning,* states: "School administrators, school boards, and teachers initiate restrictions, often with success because of their positions within the school. Librarians are not immune from being influenced by attempts to restrict access. In spite of strong verbal acceptance of the principles stated in the 'Library Bill of Rights' . . . librarians differ widely in professional practices assuring unrestricted access to information in libraries" (McDonald 1993, 5).

So be calm. Nothing happens until a person returns the form filled out. The form most libraries use is fairly standard and basically asks the same questions. Again, there are many samples in the literature. Figure 6–1 is from a public library. It is nearly identical to the form for the school library. Figure 6–2 is an example of a form used in a school district.

If your challenge is by a local group, you will be more effective if you have some basic information: ask for or find out the name and contact person of the group, the composition of the membership, if you can get on the mailing list, and if it is affiliated with any national group. You might also avail yourself of the library's resources and find newspaper stories about the group.

There may be cases where the material that is being challenged is on the Internet. Many libraries are noting in their policies that complaints about objectionable material found on the Internet should be directed to the producer of the information. The Alaska State Library Electronic Doorway (http://sled.alaska.edu/Index.html) posts the following message on the introductory screen:

FIGURE 6–1   Patron's Opinion of Library Materials
(Reprinted with permission of the Fort Vancouver Regional Library.)

PATRON'S OPINION OF LIBRARY MATERIALS

Your Name _____

Your Address _____

Title _____

Author _____

1.   What do you believe this material is about?

2.   What do you object to in the material? (Please be specific; cite pages, etc.)

3.   Why do you object to the material?

4.   All titles in the Fort Vancouver Regional Library's collection have been selected within the Library's Policy for the Selection and Discarding of Materials (attached to this form). Have you read this material? ❑Yes ❑No. Do you believe that the material falls outside the policy? If so, please explain why.

5.   What action do you wish the Library to take?

6.   Are you usually able to find what you want in the Library? _____ If not, what materials would you like to be able to find in the Library collection?

If you have any questions about the Library's Selection Policy contact the **Chair, Collection Review Committee, Fort Vancouver Regional Library,** 1007 E. Mill Plain Blvd., Vancouver, WA 98663. (206) 695-1561
1993

JUNEAU SCHOOL DISTRICT

10014 Crazy Horse Drive • Juneau, Alaska 99801 • (907) 586-2303

FIGURE 6–2 Citizens Request for Re-Evaluation of Materials/Subject Matter
(Reprinted with permission of the Juneau School District.)

Program Form #1240A

Citizens Request for Re-Evaluation of Materials/Subject Matter
At _____**School**

Request initiated by: _____

Telephone:_____ Mailing address: _____

Representing: _____ Self _____ Organization or group

Material questioned: Book-Film-Etc. _____

Author/Publisher _____ Copyright date _____

Subject Matter: (Please describe) _____

_____

Please respond to the following questions. If sufficient space is not provided, please attach additional information.

1. Have you read or considered this material/subject matter in its entirety? _____

2. To what do you object? Please cite specific content, pages, etc._____
    _____

3. What do you feel might result from the use of this material/subject matter? _____
    _____

4. What do believe is the main idea of this material/subject matter? _____
    _____

5. What reviews of this material/subject matter have you read? _____
    _____

6. For what other age group might this be suitable? _____

7. What action do you recommend the school take on this material/subject matter? _____
    _____

8. In its place, what material/subject matter do you recommend? _____

Date: _____ Signature:

SLED does not warrant this information to be accurate, authoritative, factual, or timely. The availability of networked information via SLED does not constitute endorsement of the content of that information by SLED or members of the Alaska Library Network. IF YOU FEEL THAT INFORMATION YOU HAVE OBTAINED VIA SLED OR OTHER INFORMATION SERVERS ACCESSIBLE THROUGH SLED IS INACCURATE OR OFFENSIVE, WE SUGGEST YOU CONTACT THE ORIGINAL PRODUCER/DISTRIBUTOR OF THAT INFORMATION.

When a patron brings back a reconsideration form, he or she initiates the policy's remaining steps. Notify your director or administrator, who, in turn, should inform the governing board. There may be cases where the library director or school superintendent does not accept the request for reconsideration. If, however, the request is for material owned by the library, the next step concerns the committee.

THE RECONSIDERATION COMMITTEE

The committee may be a standing committee, in which case the reconsideration form is forwarded to it. In other situations a committee is appointed for each "event." You want to make sure that your policy is clear. The Juneau (Alaska) School District reconsideration procedures, written in 1987, called for a committee of five individuals consisting of two staff members who are knowledgeable in the field of concern, the principal of the school, and two members of the community. This was interpreted by the superintendent and principals to mean that there need not be a librarian on the committee—a surprise to the librarians, who had always assumed that at least one librarian would be on any reconsideration committee. Some committees, particularly in public libraries, are composed entirely of librarians; others may be broadly based and include teachers, parents, principals, and librarians. A standing committee is preferable to an ad hoc committee. The major benefits are that the librarians can educate other members of the committee on intellectual freedom principles before any incident occurs and that there is less chance of accusation that the committee was "stacked" against the person making the complaint.

The reconsideration committee has six basic responsibilities:

1. Read, listen to, or view, in its entirety, the challenged material. If the material is something from the Internet

that the library or school district makes available, the committee will need a computer to view and read the challenged material.

2. Obtain and read all of the reviews of the material at the time of publication of the item.

3. Read and discuss the library or school district's criteria for selection and any other pertinent policies or procedures, as well as the selection process.

4. Discuss the challenged material as a group, inviting specialists such as school nurses or counselors and the librarian if he or she is not on the committee. The committee may or may not want to invite the complainant to talk with it.

5. Make a recommendation in writing to the library director or principal on the outcome of the discussion. The recommendation choices are retain, remove, restrict, or reclassify. Some members of the committee may submit a minority opinion.

6. Notify the complainant of the committee's decision and provide information about any appeal procedures. This step may be done by the committee or it may be done by the library director or superintendent, depending on the procedures in place.

As a librarian, be prepared to answer questions you may be asked by parents, administrators, or the reconsideration committee:

- Why was this book selected for your library?
- Do you have copies of reviews?
- How often was the book checked out?
- What is the usage/circulation pattern for this book?
- Do other libraries in your area have this book?
- Have there been challenges to the book in other areas?
- Why do you think this book is valuable for your collection?

Whether or not you serve on the reconsideration committee, you can have an impact on the committee's work. Statements such as this one from ALA's *Intellectual Freedom Manual* should be in the introductory packet to any committee.

It is critical that the review process be as objective as possible. If the challenged material does not meet the library's own criteria for selection (assuming, of course, that those criteria themselves are consistent with the principles of intellectual freedom), the library must be ready to acknowledge that the material is indeed unsuitable and withdraw it from the collection. If, on the other hand, as is most often the case, the material does meet the selection criteria and is deemed suitable for the collection, it is the responsibility of the library staff to respond to the complaint clearly and precisely. This response should also inform the complainant how to pursue the matter further (American Library Association 1992, 218).

It is important to view the material as a whole rather than focusing on sections that may be offensive to some. Personal, religious, political, or social views of committee members must not be used to determine whether or not material is retained. There needs to be someone who monitors the process, whether formally or informally, to ensure that policy and procedures are followed. If no one is officially doing this, it is another job that rests on the librarian's shoulders and one that should be taken seriously, particularly if no librarian is on the committee. The librarian should also be the self-appointed resource person on intellectual freedom.

THE RECONSIDERATION HEARING

Depending on your policy, there may or may not be hearings. In some public libraries an internal committee makes a recommendation to the director and the director makes a decision and announces it. In others, a committee may meet and report its recommendation to the director, the director makes a decision, and, if an appeal is made, it goes to a governing body. In a school district, a hearing may be held at a local school with the committee that is making a recommendation to the superintendent. There may also be a hearing if an appeal is made to the governing board.

If your process includes hearings, prepare logistically and emotionally. You might expect four people and have three hundred show up.

Implicitly, reconsideration hearings are a very negative process for librarians and library supporters. Depending on what your policy says, you can mitigate this aspect by encouraging community members who are in favor of the challenged material and intellectual freedom principles to speak.

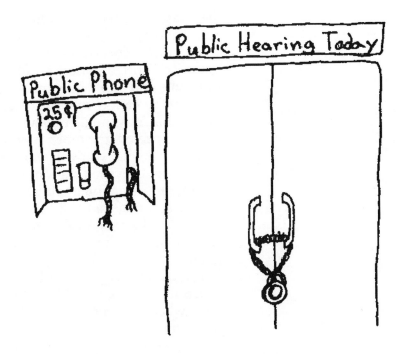

The public is getting ripped off.

A small hearing might be the committee and ten or twelve community members. It may or may not be advertised widely. An administrator who wants to keep a censorship challenge "quiet" may inform only a few people. (If you live in a state or city with open meeting laws, all meetings are open.) But keeping a hearing quiet may ultimately backfire. The Juneau School District had challenges on the same book at four different schools. The hearing at the first school had about 15 people; the second one had 400. Community members were angry because they did not know about the first hearing and have the opportunity to speak at their own school.

Public hearings are held all the time—by cities, counties, states, and agencies of the federal government. The larger the hearing, the more preparation and organization is needed. There are three basic parts: preplanning, the logistics for the hearing itself, and plans related to the final decision.

PREPLANNING

If you decide to hold a hearing, keep several key points in mind. Be organized and ensure that you publicize the date and time of the hearing in writing to committee members, parents, teachers, the board, and the media. Include information about opportunities to testify both in person and in writing. Those who filed reconsideration forms should receive a written notice inviting them to testify. Written notices should set limits on length of testimony so people will know how much (or little) to prepare. Set a beginning and an ending time. The hearing should be the only item on the evening's agenda. A commonsense rule is that the larger the crowd expected, the more attention needs to be paid to logistics. Invite the media; you will want them there. Be sure that each radio station, television station, and newspaper is sent news releases or other information about the hearing—and the name of a contact person they can call to arrange to set up in advance. If you have a local public radio station, try to arrange for it to broadcast the hearing live and to publicize this in advance to the community.

The committee or board will have to make decisions in advance about the order of speaking, what materials to have at the door, what equipment is needed (microphones), and the set-up of the room.

At this point, librarians need to find supporters to speak. Those who object to the material will be there in force. This is their opportunity to speak. Beat the bushes and gather people to talk about the freedom to read and the First Amendment. Obvious choices are educators, students, parents, attorneys, ministers, and people from the media. Ministers from mainstream churches tend to be more liberal regarding intellectual freedom. Contact community members who belong to churches where you think the minister might speak out. Asking a church member to contact the minister may be more successful than calling yourself.

When people arrive they will sign up to speak. This is also the point to pass out copies of the Library Bill of Rights, your selection policy and reconsideration procedures, and the ground rules for the hearing. Ensure that everyone has the same information and that there is an official timekeeper.

LOGISTICS

The reconsideration committee chair (or the president of the governing board) will preside over the hearing. This duty includes beginning and ending the meeting on time, announcing that the committee or board will not be making a decision the night of the hearing, and announcing when the decision will be made. Explanations about process are a necessary beginning so everyone knows the rules. The chair will inform people how long they have to speak and what order they will testify in. Choices for speaking order include: all supporters of the challenge at the beginning and all supporters of the material and intellectual freedom at the end, all who filed reconsideration forms first, an "against" and then a "for" until the list is complete, or in order of sign-up. Ask speakers to identify themselves and what organization they represent.

The chair must insist that the audience be respectful of the person speaking—and never allow the audience to vote whether or not they would like to retain or remove an item. Given the situation, such a vote might be overwhelmingly in favor of removing. Censorship challenges are not decided by popular vote. The chairperson must have the authority and option, after appropriate warnings, to discontinue the hearing if the rules are disregarded or blatantly ignored. Recessing the hearing is another option for gaining control. In no case should the chair allow speakers to give up their time to other speakers. At one Juneau hearing eight people who were signed up to speak all jumped up to give their time to another speaker who demanded that the chair give him more time. He then had the opportunity to talk for over 25 minutes, which he did. If there is any reason to suspect that the hearing might get "ugly," consider hiring security. And finally, if you guessed wrong about the time limit for the hearing, and there are still speakers on the list, make alternative arrangements to ensure that everybody who wants to testify can.

Provide a good microphone and podium so that people giving testimony can have a place to put their papers. Ensure that the audience, as well as the committee, can hear the person giving the testimony, and that the audience can hear the committee chair. You will want to tape the hearing and keep minutes.

And librarians—where should you be? Sitting in the front row, facing the committee, looking calm and composed, talking with all who have come to testify before the hearing begins. Make yourselves visible. Take—and make—opportunities to talk with the media. This is another chance to get out your message about the importance of access to information.

Your reconsideration policy and procedures will probably not cover all these details. Your library or school may never have held a hearing before. You may be making these decisions for the first time. Seek advice from others who have had public hearings, and read Dr. Janet L. Jones, *No Right Turn*. Jones has written an excellent chapter on "survival tips" for conducting a hearing in a school district. Her advice can be used in any kind of setting.

THE FINAL DECISION

At the end of the reconsideration process the committee will come to a recommendation. The decision on whether to accept, reject, or modify the committee's recommendation will be in the hands of the school superintendent or library director. His or her decision may be challenged according to the appeal process, either by a person who seeks to retain the material or one who seeks to remove it. The "moment of truth"—retain, restrict, reclassify or remove—may occur more than once through the appeal process. The final decision rests with the governing board. If there wasn't a public hearing at the committee level, there may be one at the board level. At the end you may be elated or disappointed—but you will certainly be glad it is over. However the decision goes, this is not a personal decision. It is the democratic process in action.

In many reconsideration procedures, the final step, particularly if an item was removed from the collection, is a lawsuit. If a suit is filed, particularly if you have been directly involved with the selection of the item, it is important to keep all of your files and notes. You may be called as a witness in the initial proceedings.

REFERENCES

American Library Association, Office for Intellectual Freedom. *Intellectual Freedom Manual.* 4th ed. Chicago: American Library Association, 1992.

American Library Association. Office for Intellectual Freedom. "OIF Censorship Database 1994." Chicago: American Library Association, 1995.

Jones, Janet L. *No Right Turn: Assuring the Forward Progress of Public Education.* Washington Education Association, 1993.

Juneau [Alaska] School District. Board of Education. "Rules and Regulations: Program; 1240R." Juneau, AK: August, 1987.

McDonald, Frances Beck. *Censorship and Intellectual Freedom: A Survey of School Librarians' Attitudes and Moral Reasoning.* Metuchen, NJ: Scarecrow Press, 1993.

Minnesota Coalition Against Censorship. *Selection Policies and Reevaluation Procedures: A Workbook.* Stillwater, MN: Minnesota Educational Media Organization, 1991.

Schexnaydre, Linda, Nancy Burns, and the Emporia State University School of Library and Information Management. *Censorship: A Guide for Successful Workshop Planning.* Phoenix, AZ: Oryx Press, 1984.

7 A RECONSIDERATION CASE STUDY: *DADDY'S ROOMMATE*

This case study of an actual reconsideration situation that occured in the Juneau School District is written by Ann K. Symons, librarian at Juneau Douglas High School. It presents actions leading up to the challenges, the actual steps that happened, the reaction of the librarians and the community at large, the coverage in the local media, and the experiences of the librarians in the school district.

(Reprinted with the permission of Alyson Publications. Illustration by Michael Willhoite.)

In January 1994, *School Library Journal* reported on a censorship challenge in Juneau, Alaska, over the children's book *Daddy's Roommate* by Michael Willhoite. Anne Penway, assistant director of ALA's Office for Intellectual Freedom, remarked that the school challenge in Juneau was the first time a particular book had been challenged on such a wide level. It was one of the year's major censorship cases. In addition, it was also one of the biggest news stories in the Alaskan capital in 1993.

The story has a happy ending. On November 17, 1993, the Board of Education of the Juneau School District voted 7–1 to retain *Daddy's Roommate* in all elementary schools. Individual members of the board spoke eloquently in defense of intellectual freedom and the selection policy and of the right of the librarian to develop a diverse collection, and affirmed the good judgment shown by the librarians in selecting this book. The vote of the Juneau school board also affirmed the superintendent's recommendation to retain the book. The meeting was broadcast live on public radio. The librarians sat in the first row, savoring every word of the positive message sent that night. At the end we wanted to jump up and down, cheer, and hug each other, but we waited patiently until we went out to a local restaurant to celebrate.

The *Daddy's Roommate* "case" neither began nor ended with the board's vote. For many of us it began in library school with a commitment to intellectual freedom, to serving a diverse community, and to providing all points of view in our libraries. Who knows where it will end . . .

In the 23 years that I have been a school librarian in the Juneau School District we had *never* had a formal challenge to any material in any school. Rarely had any of the eight school librarians even sat down with a parent who had a concern. Censorship in Juneau—couldn't happen here, we said!

In late September 1993 during Banned Books Week and at the beginning of a long struggle, I wrote an e-mail message to a friend. It was the beginning of a journal that never materialized.

Tomorrow I promise I will start a journal. A parent was in my office today accusing me of promoting sodomy and bestiality. He was angry that I showed the book [*Daddy's Roommate*] in his daughter's American Government class. They were studying the Bill of Rights. All the kids in the class were high school seniors—17 and 18 years old. He was definitely civil, just angry. He got angrier when I told him we had other books about homosexuality in our library at the high school.

When you take censorship out of the abstract where it stays most of the time, it's a horse of a different color. It's fine to talk in [ALA] Council about how much we support the freedom to read, abhor censorship—but when it comes to your door it's ugly.

There are also the positive aspects. When I got back from the American Government class today there was a letter of support on my desk from a woman who had grown up in a lesbian household. She wrote of how much she appreciated our efforts to provide age appropriate materials which showed alternative lifestyle families. She had never had any of these growing up and wrote about how alienated she felt.

A radio reporter came in to talk to me today to make an appointment to do a story on Monday. Somehow—probably because none of the elementary librarians want to step out front—I'm the one the media calls. The reporter went to a meeting she knew was happening at a Baptist Church last night and they asked her to leave. It was a strategy meeting.

The school librarians are doing great. They are all under a lot of pressure. The [reconsideration] committee meetings at individual schools start soon—and we look forward to getting their decisions to the superintendent. Enough—I'm sure I've bored your ear off. Obviously my life seems consumed by this event. Cheers, Ann

Juneau, the capital of Alaska, is a small, highly educated community of about 28,000 citizens. It is a liberal community with a visible gay/lesbian population. Children of gays and lesbians attend every school in our community. Thus it was not at all surprising that each elementary librarian made the decision to purchase *Daddy's Roommate*. Did we know there would be a challenge? Probably. Did we know that we would unleash a highly organized protest by the religious right and that we would see bigotry, discrimination, and hatred directed at one group of citizens in the community? Absolutely not. We had no idea.

There was no opportunity for informal dialogue with parents about censorship and "the book." Reconsideration forms were filed before librarians got the books out of the box and on the shelves. All of the negative things you read about when the censor comes happened. And it is scary.

What you don't often read about in library literature is that positive things happen too. The librarians "bonded" together, never wavered from our course of protecting the freedom to read, worked together, and supported each other. We took every opportunity to put our message forward, no matter what the question or event. We all fell into roles—I turned out to be the spokesperson to the media and our link to ALA/OIF. Others met with parents. We all sought support from local groups.

Ultimately it was our policies that saved us. Unfortunately, it was not the selection policy but the Juneau School District's policy on controversial issues and antidiscrimination. There was no board-approved selection policy.

Attacks on the Freedom to Learn: 1993–94 Report cited the Juneau decision as part of a disturbing trend to reclassify books into a different section of the collection. Part of the decision by the superintendent and school board did indeed involve putting the book in the Family section of nonfiction. Retaining the book and keeping access to it open were the most important parts of the Juneau school board vote. However, the board sent a greater message to the community the night of November 16—that it would not tolerate bigotry and discrimination in the Juneau School District.

This case wasn't about *Daddy's Roommate*. It was over a clash in values: who determines what a child shall read and who selects books for school libraries. It was about discrimination and about providing diverse collections, protecting the right of children to read, and parental responsibility for one's own children.

The following chronology presents some of the events along the way that shaped the outcome of the censorship challenge.

CHRONOLOGY OF A CENSORSHIP INCIDENT: MARCH 1993–OCTOBER 1994

March 1993

School librarians in a regular monthly meeting read, review, and discuss *Daddy's Roommate* and *Families*. Each librarian decides to purchase a copy for her elementary school library.

High school librarian orders five copies of *Daddy's Roommate* and *Families* from high school money, as agreed by the librarians.

July 1993

Robert Van Slyke, superintendent of schools, calls to say that he has all the copies of *Daddy's Roommate* on his desk. Was I aware of this title? Did I know that adding this to our library collections would cause a problem in the community? We agreed that I would talk with the librarians about his concerns and that he would send me the books.

August 1993

Books arrive at school; "offending pages" are marked with small yellow Post-it notes.

Librarians meet before school starts and affirm that they had valid reasons for selecting the book and that they will put it in the collections. No one talks about where to classify the book. Librarians do not know who put the Post-it notes on the pages or how the book got from receiving to the superintendent instead of following the regular receiving pattern. Librarians surmise that someone in the school district's mail room objected to the book, put the notes on the pages, and sent the box to the superintendent.

September 1993

Twenty-one people file reconsideration forms at Juneau Public Library seeking to remove *Daddy's Roommate* from the public library's collection. The reconsideration committee meets and reviews the materials. Juneau Public Library writes complainants informing them that the committee's decision is to retain the material and move the book to the nonfiction section of the libraries.

With censorship you don't quite get the whole picture

An ad hoc organization, People for Responsible Education (P.R.E.), forms to remove the book from school libraries. Organizing meetings are held in local churches. Flyers informing parents about *Daddy's Roommate* are distributed in churches and day-care centers.

Juneau Douglas High School celebrates Banned Books Week with exhibits, class projects, mock trials. *Daddy's Roommate* purchased for high school library, taken to twelfth grade American government class, which is discussing the First Amendment. Student calls parent, who arrives at school 30 minutes after the class to express displeasure that a book portraying sodomy was shown to his daughter. Parent complains to principal, superintendent, school board president.

First of numerous reconsideration forms begin to arrive at local schools.

October 1993

Attend Juneau Education Association school reps meeting to seek support for upcoming challenge based on NEA national policies on censorship. Listen to school board candidate answer questions about *Daddy's Roommate*.

Call all school board candidates to ask them views on *Daddy's Roommate*. One in support, three against. Two candidates win— one for and one against.

Juneau Empire (October 10, 1993) publishes editorial: "Presenting all points of view; Libraries shouldn't ban books." (See Appendix B).

Reconsideration forms continue to be turned in at local schools (by the droves); some community members have heard that you won't get to speak if you haven't turned in a form. Supporters of intellectual freedom devise a way to use the form to support the book.

Parent involved in P.R.E sends five-page letter of questions/requests for information on meetings to decide to purchase *Daddy's Roommate*, reviews, criteria, documents on how book meets criteria in selection guidelines, descriptions of objectivity of author, etc., to elementary school principal. The letter also asked the school district to provide any "inspections or audits which confirm [the] claim that the librarians abide by the recommendation of ALA's Code of Ethics." Letter asks that this be considered "a request pursuant to the Freedom of Information Act." Referred to superintendent.

Petitions are circulated, members of P.R.E. canvass door-to-door asking if librarians should select books, flyers are put in mail-

Reviews of *Daddy's Roommate*

Willhoite, Michael. *Daddy's Roommate*, illus. by author. Boston: Alyson, 1990. ISBN 1-55583-178-8; LC 90-45593.

Advocate, August 13, 1991, p. 85

Booklist, March 1, 1991, p. 1403

Bulletin of the Center for Children's Books, March 1991, p. 182

Horn Book, July 1990, p. 56

Publishers Weekly, December 7, 1990, p. 80

School Library Journal, April 1991, p. 105–106

Small Press Book Review, May 1991, p. 6

boxes without postage. P.R.E. contends that "school can and must bring up issue of respect, tolerance and differences, but at an age appropriate level. . . . Our rights to protect our children from harmful social pressures have been taken away."

Committees appointed by superintendent at three schools. One school decides that it will use its site council as the reconsideration committee regardless of what policy says. First meeting occurs between the committee and the complainants. The meeting was not publicized. Twelve parents, three librarians and four committee members attend. Librarian was not invited to be a member of the reconsideration committee at any school. Committee recommends retaining book and moving it to nonfiction (October 7).

Second school site council meets as reconsideration committee and holds public hearing for complainants to speak. Librarian acts as consultant to the committee. Four hundred parents and interested community members attend hearing which has the feel of a religious revival meeting. Chairperson has a difficult time maintaining control of the meeting. Speakers are allowed to give up time to other speakers (October 12).

Third school reconsideration committee meets, also as formal public hearing. The reconsideration committee is chaired by the principal. Two hundred fifty people attend. Many speakers are the same as the previous evening (October 13).

Both schools make the same decision as school one. These three recommendations are forwarded to the superintendent.

Twenty middle school students file reconsideration forms for the book at the elementary school next door; middle school librarian's car is vandalized.

Fourth school has challenges but waits to see what happens; no hearing held; no reconsideration committee appointed.

No challenge filed at school five.

Numerous letters to the editor appear in the *Juneau Empire*.

Juneau Douglas High School students introduce resolution at Alaska Association of Student Governments. Resolution condemning censorship and banning of literary materials passes.

Librarians meet weekly; high school librarian takes on task of dealing with the media, writing testimony, being contact person with ALA Office for Intellectual Freedom, which provides case support. Other librarians divide up other jobs. Librarians realize that the Juneau school board has no approved library materials selection policy, although it has controversial issues policy, anti-discrimination policy, and reconsideration policy.

High school English classes work on censorship project; assignment is to write testimony for hearings. Several students eventually testify before Juneau school board in November.

People for Responsible Education organizes a school boycott. Two hundred students stay home during the one-day boycott.

Superintendent Robert S. Van Slyke sends memo (October 25; see Appendix B) to complainants, proponents, elementary principals, and board members. Subject: Finding regarding *Daddy's Roommate*. Van Slyke states, "There is no apparent educationally sound reason for the removal of the book. Therefore, the recommendation of the three committees that have considered the work . . . be adopted and be applicable to all District elementary schools."

November 1993

People for Responsible Education file a 20-page appeal to Van Slyke's decision (November 4).

P.R.E. appeal faxed to Judith Krug, ALA Office for Intellectual Freedom.

Juneau school librarians make up information packets for members of the Juneau school board. Packets include Library Bill of Rights, interpretation on "Access to Resources and Services in the School Library Media Program," "Free Access to Libraries for Minors," reviews of *Daddy's Roommate,* testimony by librarians from earlier hearings (November 5).

Life's Little Instruction Calendar has an appropriate message for the day: "When facing a difficult task, act as though it is impossible to fail. If you are going after Moby Dick, take along the tartar sauce" (November 9).

Judith Krug and Anne Penway (ALA, OIF) respond with comments on the P.R.E. appeal. Response is sent by librarians to the superintendent and school board (November 10).

Librarians call parents, community leaders, authors, ministers, public and university librarians, American Association of University Women, League of Women Voters' members, Juneau Education Association, Friends of Juneau Public Libraries members, and gay and lesbian organizations for support.

Anchorage television station comes to Juneau to film a segment on censorship incident for Anchorage viewers.

Alaska Public Radio and local PBS radio station do in-depth pieces on *Daddy's Roommate* challenge.

Students in University of Alaska class do a 15-minute video on incident for a class project.

Juneau school board holds public hearings on *Daddy's Roommate* appeal. District provides informational sheet that includes background, procedures, summary, and board policy on controversial issues. Each night 300–400 people attend; hearings are broadcast live on public radio. Security guards are hired for each evening but stay "out of sight" (November 10–11).

Juneau school board holds special meeting, broadcast live on public radio, to vote on appeal of *Daddy's Roommate*. A motion is introduced for "modified affirmation" of the superintendent's decision. Motion fails 7–1 with little discussion. Resolution affirming Superintendent Van Slyke's decision to retain *Daddy's Roommate* is introduced. All board members speak, several provide written justification for their vote. Board denies request of People for Responsible Education to reverse superintendent's decision on *Daddy's Roommate*. Resolution to uphold superintendent's recommendation passes 7–1 (November 10).

"My Turn" op-ed piece by Ann Symons appears in *Juneau Empire* explaining why a parent who had testified could not find the politically conservative authors he was looking for at Juneau Douglas High School Library. (November 23; see Appendix B).

Parents request that book selection be done by committee with parent majority.

Librarians review all school district policies concerning selection and reconsideration.

December 1993/January 1994

Librarians draft new policies on selection of library materials and reconsideration process and send to superintendent through curriculum director. (Librarians were not asked to write new draft policies.)

February/March 1994

School board policy committee meets to discuss draft policies on selection of materials and reconsideration process. Each meeting is attended by two or three librarians and president of the People for Responsible Education. Major issue is who has the responsibility to select books for school libraries.

Symons sends memo to school board policy committee correcting P.R.E.'s statement that ALA's Library Bill of Rights contained language about maturation levels (March 7).

Symons is requested by the superintendent to "state the name of the account used to purchase five copies of *Daddy's Roommate* and *Families*" and "to identify the origin of the funds in the account, and state the process followed in deciding to purchase those particular books" (March 8).

School librarians (all eight) respond to Superintendent Van Slyke in a memo (March 10).

April 1994

President of P.R.E. files reconsideration request for book in elementary school library, *Asking about Sex and Growing Up* by Joanna Cole. Specific objections are to chapters "Touching Feels Good," "What Is Sexual Intercourse," and "What Is Homosexuality." This book has been challenged in two school districts in Alaska in the past two years and retained in both challenges.

Superintendent Van Slyke, President of Juneau school board Dale Staley, and Juneau school librarians receive letter from Judith Krug informing them that the Partnership of the Juneau School District (librarians, superintendent, school board) has been designated by the Freedom to Read Foundation (F.T.R.F.) as recipient of its 1994 Roll of Honor Award (April 14).

Site council (14 members) acts as reconsideration committee for *Asking about Sex and Growing Up* and recommends retaining book in present classification.

Juneau school board passes new selection of educational materials and reconsideration policy. Policy is silent about who selects materials. Superintendent is requested to draft regulations/procedures for new policies.

May 1994

Juneau Empire runs editorial: "Book policy makes sense; Let the librarians do their jobs" (May 1; see Appendix B).

Superintendent's decision is to uphold site committee recommendation on Cole book.

Librarians prepare information packets for school board in case an appeal is filed over the summer. No appeal is filed.

First person to file as a school board candidate for the September election is a member of P.R.E.

June 1994

Superintendent Van Slyke, school board member Alan Schorr, and librarians Ann Symons and Marilyn Clark accept F.T.R.F. award at ALA Annual Conference, Miami.

July 1994

Superintendent has JDHS book order on his desk; wants to know if any books on the order about homosexuality are for the elementary schools.

September 1994

Friends of Juneau Public Libraries decides to host a candidates forum on intellectual freedom for Banned Books Week. School librarians help write questions.

Symons serves on JEA Pace Committee, which interviews and endorses candidates for school board and assembly. Questions on intellectual freedom are included.

School district provides access to Internet with its own Internet node and networked computers. Librarians begin drafting Internet policy for school board.

October 1994

All conservative candidates (four) lose school board election.

Alaska Civil Liberties Union presents 1994 First Amendment Award to the Alaska Library Association and the Alaska Association of School Librarians.

Life goes on!

ANALYSIS OF THE INCIDENT

FACTORS LEADING TO SUCCESS

First and foremost, Juneau is a liberal community and the school board was composed mainly of members with very liberal leanings. The Juneau school board had policies about controversial issues and against discrimination. The book was purchased for all of the elementary schools making it impossible for parents to pit one school against another. The librarians were well organized and selected one librarian to be the "leader." The librarians selected their message and were united as a group in support of the book and the principles of intellectual freedom. They attended all public meetings as a group and always sat in the front, appearing to be calm, cool, collected—and professional. All of the emotional outpouring was done by those objecting to the book.

The elementary school principals were supportive of the librarians. Librarians had been attending school board meetings regularly for several years and knew all of the board members—and the board members knew the librarians and their programs.

While there was media coverage on radio and television and letters to the editor and stories in the newspapers almost daily, the *Juneau Empire* printed a pro-intellectual freedom editorial right away. One of the librarians was in contact with ALA's Office for Intellectual Freedom from the beginning, and the school district was thus provided all the case support it needed.

The librarians used the challenge as an opportunity to get people involved. This included parents, ministers, representatives of local organizations with strong ties to intellectual freedom, and high school students. Teachers and students seized this opportunity to use the First Amendment as a part of assignments. Students testified at hearings, and they initiated a resolution with their state student government organization.

Many people in the community were offended that the issue was about homophobia, intolerance, and bigotry.

TACTICS USED BY THE CHALLENGERS

The challengers of *Daddy's Roommate* were a loosely knit coalition from various church groups. It was difficult in the end to keep the coalition together. Either by individuals or as part of the People for Responsible Education campaign, leaflets were distributed to churches and preschools, and some were put in mailboxes without postage—a federal offense. Anonymous letters were sent. Money was spent for advertising as part of an ongoing TV spot from one of the local churches.

Letters to the editor played a key role in the campaign to get rid of "the book." Using the national agenda of the religious right, opponents distorted the issue from the freedom to read to religious issues about homosexuality. A group of parents requested a list of school district teachers who are homosexuals. There were threats to take over the school board and door-to-door canvassing with petitions about who should select books.

There was pressure to change the policies and procedures on selection. On a more serious note, the car of one of the librarians was vandalized, and all of the librarians felt threatened and fearful after a very emotional public hearing with hundred of parents. There was a school boycott in which about 200 students were kept home for one day.

In the end, none of these tactics proved successful in either changing school district policies or removing the book.

In the chronology many written documents and articles are mentioned. Some of the more important supporting papers are in Appendix B. Feel free to use these materials in challenges in your community either in format or in content.

LESSONS

Participating in a full-blown censorship incident is like going to hell and returning. It consumes your life and it becomes all-important; it seems like a battle even though librarians are not at war with anybody.

What did I learn? First, that a real-life censorship challenge is not the same as learning about censorship in library school or being supportive of intellectual freedom during one's professional career. You must decide where you "really" stand on intellectual freedom, how hard you are going to work to ensure a successful outcome, and who your friends are. I learned that there are many positive aspects to a censorship challenge, including the opportunity to educate a community and a generation of high school students. It was an experience I hadn't bargained for, wouldn't wish on anybody, and wouldn't trade away for the world.

REFERENCES

Attacks on the Freedom to Learn: 1993–1994 Report. Washington, DC; People for the American Way, 1994.

"In Biggest School Challenge, Daddy's Roommate Is Staying." *School Library Journal* (January, 1994).

3 THE LIBRARIAN AND THE CENSORSHIP CHALLENGE

This nitty-gritty chapter discusses tactics librarians can use to defend the right to read if a formal challenge is filed against specific library resources. It discusses political, philosophical, and practical mechanisms both organized censors and protectors of intellectual freedom use. Dealing with the media, the community, and public hearings are discussed. The emotional climate of a challenge is dealt with realistically.

censorSHIP

In *How to Win: A Practical Guide for Defeating the Radical Right in Your Community*, compiled by the Radical Right Task Force of the National Jewish Democratic Council, Judith Krug and Anne Penway from ALA contributed the chapter on public library censorship. They say, "The most consistent thing about censors is that they are never content to regulate their own reading or that of their own children. They believe they should decide for everyone what is appropriate, and if you don't agree, you're immoral, un-American, and a lousy parent" (Krug 1994, 98). Or they might have added: a lousy librarian.

HOW TO APPROACH A CENSORSHIP CHALLENGE

Censorship is defined by the American Library Association as "the change in the access status of material, made by a governing authority or its representatives. Such changes include: exclusion, restriction, removal or age/grade level changes." ALA further defines a continuum of activities that occur during challenges that may or may not result in censorship. An *expression of concern* has judgmental overtones. One step up, the *oral complaint* questions the appropriateness of the material. Both are spoken. The *written complaint* is a formal challenge (Doyle 1994, 69).

Whether you are dealing with an expression of concern, a written, or an oral complaint, don't panic; start at step one. Unfortunately, all the policies and procedures and "preparedness" in the world aren't going to keep you from feeling besieged emotionally during a censorship challenge. Keeping a positive attitude helps, although sometimes it's hard to remember the positive parts in the midst of what seems like a crisis in your professional life. One can learn more about intellectual freedom during an intense intellectual freedom challenge than during years of workshops, conferences, professional reading, and serving on intellectual freedom committees. There will be times when you don't feel in control, when in fact you are not in control of the processes or the decision. There will be times when you feel left out, but none of the process of a censorship challenge is secret nor should any of the meetings be closed. If the process has been designed, particularly in schools, to leave you out, remember that you are "welcome" to attend all meetings.

There will be many things for you to do during a challenge. One important duty may include being on the reconsideration committee. The pace will be frazzled and frenetic because, in addition to doing your regular job and feeling besieged, you will have dozens of additional tasks if you want to help ensure that the outcome is to retain the item in question.

Throughout the period of the challenge, some librarians find it useful to keep a journal. Others find that making general notes of "things to do" after it is over is helpful. You need to ask: How did your reconsideration policy work? Where were the glitches? Does it need revision? How do you initiate that process and influence the product?

During a challenge, particularly if the item in question is for children or young adults, you will find yourself talking with parents who want to protect their children—and everybody else's children—from your harmful materials. You will find yourself doing staff training—not just for the librarians, but the whole staff, and in a school library this includes teachers and administrators. Challenges are a wonderful opportunity to educate everybody: parents, staff, community members and groups, the board, school administrators, students. It probably also isn't the time you would have picked. Now you don't have a choice.

Censorship becomes an issue for the whole staff, and the librarians must provide the leadership and the information. Take some time for personal reassurances and sympathy; bring some cookies or flowers to let your staff know you recognize their stress, too.

Relations with the media are a vital part of a censorship challenge. You will write testimony, draft letters, write press releases, and sometimes in the privacy of your car or home, you may scream!

At a time when tempers are short and you are feeling the "them against us" mentality, it is critical to treat all people involved in the process with respect. You may not agree with their values, you may not agree with their objectives to remove the material in question or to try to get you to restrict access to a particular group. A challenge, however, should not be treated like an adversarial process. Each group will use tactics it feels are important to ensure success. Many of these tactics, which will be described later, are legitimate tools of a democracy. The people who challenge library materials are patrons, community members. Librarians and library staff should treat them as all other patrons are treated—fairly and openly. Even though they may make accusations that are professionally or personally insulting, it is important to avoid being defensive—hard to do sometimes, but important. One part of the librarian's job, through leadership, will be controlling confrontation. Librarians seeking to develop their skills in dealing with confrontation should view Arch Lustberg's video *Controlling the Confrontation*, available from ALA Video Network at 800–441–8273.

So, here you are frazzled, teaching, learning, feeling bummed out that your professional judgment is in question and that you have to jump in and ensure that the outcome of the challenge will be successful. Will it? You have a big role to play here. Stop and ask yourself some of the questions on the list below. Thinking about, and writing down, responses to the questions below will help clarify your handling of the situation, although the answers might not come easily.

- Am I overreacting?
- Is the answer too inflexible?
- Do I know enough about the person making the complaints?
- Do I know the relevant laws?
- Am I familiar with the materials?
- Is there a hidden agenda?
- Do I know the reasons why this material was originally selected?
- Am I getting defensive?
- Am I promising more than I can deliver?
- Is my answer too simplistic?
- Have I identified the real issues?
- Is my body language consistent with my oral response?
- Does my response put the patron in a no-win situation?
- Am I leaving myself any alternatives?
- Is the patron open to other suggestions?
- Have I respected the patron's value system?

- Is my professional judgment being challenged?
- Are my personal values being challenged?
- Is this part of an organized effort?
- Do others have information that would help?
- Is the concern of the patron for his or her child only?
- Do I know the library's collection development policy?

(Intellectual Freedom Manual [Alaska] 1985).

Judith Krug has worked at the American Library Association for over thirty years, most of those years as director of the Office for Intellectual Freedom. In many presentations she has remarked that "no one is ever alone in a censorship battle." Each librarian, during a censorship battle, will (and should) find a support group. Whether this is other librarians in your community, an e-mail friend from the OIF listserv, or people outside the library field, make sure that you have someone to talk to who understands intellectual freedom principles and with whom you can try out ideas.

Think about your own bottom line; for everyone it is different. Some librarians are willing to put their job on the line for intellectual freedom, others are not. If you find yourself uncomfortable defending something you don't agree with, ask another librarian to do it for you.

THE LIBRARIAN'S RESPONSIBILITIES DURING A CENSORSHIP CHALLENGE

Will you be successful in retaining library materials that have been challenged?

A study done in Wisconsin by Dianne McAfee Hopkins asked the question, "What are the factors that are most likely to influence the outcome of challenges to the school library media materials found in public schools?"

The answer:

- How recently a materials selection policy has been approved or if the policy has never been approved;
- How a policy is used during a challenge, especially non-use;
- Educational level of the library media specialist, with those with master's degrees or above reporting higher rates of retention;

- The role of the principal, with highest retention of materials relating to the library media specialist's view of the principal as being supportive during the challenge;
- The role of teachers, with high retention of materials relating to the library media specialists' view of teachers as supportive during the challenge;
- Level of active support for removal with least likelihood of retention when parents and school board members actively support removal;
- Outside assistance provided by the Cooperative Children's Book Center, with higher retention rates for those using CCBC's intellectual freedom service [available only to those in Wisconsin]
- Who initiates challenges, with challenges initiated by school board members(s) or parent(s) more likely to result in retention of material than those initiated by officials and staff inside the school (Hopkins 1990, 229).

This study gives us a springboard to use common sense in dealing with a challenge. Have a materials selection policy, use it during a challenge, get the support of your principal and teachers, and understand that it is just as important for those "inside the system"—principals and teachers—to follow procedures as it is for those outside. Get help from anywhere you can: from ALA's Office for Intellectual Freedom, your state intellectual freedom committee, and your professional colleagues. It all helps in determining the outcome of a challenge.

Let the process work and be an advocate for intellectual freedom every step of the way. A school board candidate remarked during a recent challenge that the relationship between the schools and the community was a precious commodity and that we needed to pick our battles carefully. He felt that the book challenge wasn't that worthy a battle and that the librarians had used poor judgment in selecting the book. As this illustrates, there will be times when you will be disappointed in reactions from people you thought were library supporters. You will also meet people that you didn't know felt so passionately about the First Amendment and their right and their children's right to read. Applaud them and be sure to get their names and phone numbers for the next fight.

Very early on in a censorship challenge, sit down and figure out what your message is. It should have no more than three key points and will involve protecting the right to read, listen, view, etc. If this is an issue involving youth materials, one part of the message may be that "parents have the right and responsibility to choose what their children read or do not read, but that they do not have the right to make these decisions for other people's children." Don't feel that you have to write the message yourself—you can "borrow" it from ALA, from AASL, or from anything written about censorship that speaks to what you want to say.

Read the following paragraph put out by American Association of School Librarians, a division of the American Library Association. Note that its three key points have been emphasized here to illustrate the message.

> The school library media program **serves all of the students of the community**—not only those children of the most powerful, the most vocal or even the majority, but **all of the students** who attend school. The collection includes materials to meet the needs of all learners . . . including those from a diversity of backgrounds. The school **library program strives to maintain a diverse collection that represents various points of view** on current and historical topics, as well as a wide variety of areas of interest to all students served. **Though one parent or member of the school community may feel a particular title in the school library media center's collection is inappropriate, others will feel the title is not only appropriate but desirable** (American Association of School Librarians 1990).

If you are going to testify, write out what you are going to say. Just as your message should contain no more than three key points, make sure there are no more than three points in your testimony. If you have handouts for the reconsideration committee, the school board, or the library board, also give them to the media. Use a strong clear voice and be ready to answer questions.

Seek out and contact other professional groups, like your local chapter of the National Education Association or the National Council of Teachers of English that are traditionally associated with strong concerns about intellectual freedom. Their support will be important as a censorship incident escalates. Educate every group that you can, both formally and informally.

Not being intimidated is important, and it is vital that librarians stand up and be counted. Don't compromise; it is better to lose than compromise, especially if compromise means agreeing to a precedent for restricted access or labeling. Be strong, be firm, and say what you believe. If people expect you to be intimidated, to compromise, or to agree to either restrict access to materials or to ensure that certain people don't get to check out material, prove them wrong.

You may find that there are only one or two copies of the challenged item in town. Get as many copies of the book (or magazine, article, etc.) into the public's hands as soon as possible. Ask the bookstore to order copies, borrow copies from other libraries, and ask the publisher for a few free copies if necessary. A librarian who had recently been through a challenge suggested to others on the ALAOIF listserv that if you just can't get any copies, ask the publisher for permission to photocopy the book for the reconsideration committee, agreeing to destroy the copies at the end of the challenge. Recently, a children's publisher in New York sent the Juneau (Alaska) School District 25 paperback copies of a book being challenged. The person filing the reconsideration form thought he had the only copy and kept it in his briefcase, bringing it out to show selected excerpts at public meetings. In the meantime, the librarians had enough copies to distribute to every school nurse, counselor, school board member and the entire reconsideration committee, so all of those people had the opportunity to view the work as a whole and form their own opinions.

In summary, the responsibilities of the librarian during a challenge will be:

- Provide support to the reconsideration committee (whether you are on the committee or not, and whether or not you are asked);
- Provide background information and reviews and information about whether or not this material has been challenged before and the outcome;
- Keep the book in circulation during the challenge;
- Attend meetings;
- Use the opportunity to educate people about intellectual freedom and the library's policies and procedures;
- Write testimony;
- Deal with the media;
- Get more copies of the book;
- Prepare packets for parent groups, others in the community, the school board or library board;
- Form a support group of librarians;
- Keep a record of everything that happens during the censorship incident; all press clippings, TV clips, radio interviews and coverage, memos, letters to the editor, official school district documents, i.e., superintendent's decision, board members' statements, reconsideration forms, etc.; and
- Don't forget to breathe!

Seek advice—there is plenty available. Your first stops should be your state's intellectual freedom committee, ALA's Office for Intellectual Freedom which will provide case support, and the American Civil Liberties Union. Books and magazine articles about censorship often provide very helpful hints in dealing with challenges.

In the midst of a crisis, always be calm and courteous. Never let this be seen as an adversarial process; share all information about your policies and procedures. Be respectful of the process and of the individual(s) who are challenging materials in the library.

DEALING WITH THE MEDIA

One of the more difficult parts of living through a censorship challenge is dealing with the media. The first rule is to be prepared and know the facts of the censorship incident. Again, be calm, not emotional.

Librarians are not expected to be in the middle of the road on censorship issues. Know your message, tailor it to your library and to the situation at hand, and always stick to your message. Articulate your position clearly and move the discussion to a higher level whenever you can, focusing on intellectual freedom and the freedom to read.

Generally, the media is your friend, especially on intellectual freedom and First Amendment issues. News articles will generally be balanced; the media looks for controversy and will tell both sides because stories with conflict sell. Editorials are another matter. At the same time a paper is providing news stories that you may think show "your side" inadequately, it may write an editorial supporting the importance of intellectual freedom.

Some basic tips for dealing with the media are:

- Ensure that the media are informed and that the information you give them is accurate.
- Provide the press with materials on basic intellectual freedom principles and issues, starting with the First Amendment.
- Send material to the paper's editor as well as to reporters.
- If you don't know the answer to a question, be honest and say you don't know.
- If you agree to get back to a reporter with an answer, make sure that you follow through.
- Be credible.
- Keep the media informed. You can phone, fax, and send press releases.

- Generate more media coverage with letters to the editor about the story from supporters.
- Don't say "no comment" or this is "off the record." If you can't release information, say so. Off-the-record comments might be used, even if you are assured that they won't be.
- Role-play with friends. Practice answering the tough questions, always keeping in mind the message you want to convey.
- Make sure that all librarians in your group are saying the same things.
- Never repeat a negative, never give a one-word answer, and stay in control by moving the discussion to what you want to talk about.

Try to think of all the questions you might be asked, and prepare convincing responses in advance. Never walk in unprepared to a meeting with a reporter. The same is true for a telephone interview or a radio or television appearance. Ask ALA's Office for Intellectual Freedom to send you "A Guide to Working with the Media." Full of good general advice and tips to help you, this will be a publication you can use for general library advocacy. ALA's Public Information Office can also provide general information about working with the media, and media training for librarians is often available at ALA conferences.

TACTICS IN A CENSORSHIP CHALLENGE

Some tactics encountered during a censorship challenge are practiced every day by thousands of people who lobby, are perfectly legal, and are a part of the democratic process. Some tactics may be used to intimidate, and some may be illegal. Report those that are illegal, such as threats, to the police.

TACTICS USED BY BOTH SIDES
The tactics discussed below are legal and are used every day as part of the democratic process to influence officials in their decision making. Some of the tactics are more likely to be used by those wishing to restrict access to material; others are used equally by both groups.

One easy way to reach people is to disseminate information. This can be done by distributing mass leaflets or mass mailings.

Schools, school districts, and public libraries or public library friends groups often have newsletters sent through the mail that can carry the library's message. An example of a mass mailing letter is at the end of the chapter. To avoid postal costs, many groups give out leaflets in local churches. Local telephone calls are free; they only take time. Many groups use telephone trees or phone banks to reach many people at a time with key information, such as the date, time, and place and an invitation to attend a hearing.

Many groups also form coalitions with other organizations that may wish the same outcome. Some coalitions, such as the Minnesota Coalition Against Censorship, have been around for a long time; others form on the spur of the moment and are gone when a challenge ends.

Letters to the editor get a wide readership. Libraries and challengers can both give information to the media through press releases sent by fax or e-mail or dropped off at a newspaper, radio or TV station office. The telephone call to a reporter can also be useful. Some groups pay to advertise. Nonprofit organizations can send in public service announcements to the media.

Contacting local groups, offering to come to meetings and speak and answer questions, can be an effective technique. You may find that your "opponent" is there as well, bringing his or her message in an attempt to influence local politics. Be sure to plant questions from the audience that you want to answer. As mentioned earlier, getting to know board members and regularly attending school board and library board meetings is useful. Many board members pay attention to information coming from someone they know. Speaking of boards, there may be pressure either from librarians or parents/community members to change library policies. Testifying at public hearings can be a way to bring your message once again.

None of the above techniques will be very useful if nobody has read the material being challenged. Both groups may seek to distribute the book or other materials. Librarians want community members to see a work in its entirety. Often would-be censors want people to only see the "bad parts."

Use ALA intellectual freedom materials, and don't be at all surprised that the would-be censor has all the ALA material you have. He or she may seek to put a different interpretation on it than you will or ALA does.

Petitions, protests, picketing, and boycotts are popular attention-getting devices. And often just sheer persistence pays off. The threat of legal action always seems to hang overhead.

TACTICS USED BY THE WOULD-BE CENSOR

There are some tactics that are used mainly by the would-be censor. Photocopying and filing many reconsideration forms against the same book can be used in an attempt to overwhelm the library. Letters, often distributed widely in churches, may talk about threats to children, whether it is an adult book, like Madonna's *Sex*, or a book published for children. Key points often used are that tax dollars are being spent on something objectionable and the material is not appropriate for youth. In their letters, adults are encouraged to "get involved" by seeking to remove items from the library. These tactics can be combatted in the same way—getting information out to community members.

Groups wanting to restrict access to library materials often distort the issues and the facts. They may try to take over school boards, library boards, or school site councils by getting their candidates elected. Those seeking to disrupt the work flow of a school district or library may "drop in" to see the library director, the principal, or the superintendent and demand information or time—or that the librarians be fired. Demands for unreasonable amounts of information may be made. Some parents will challenge the diversity of the library's collection by counting the number of books on "each side" of a topic—pro abortion/anti-abortion, pro homosexuality/anti-homosexuality—to make a point.

There may be a growing number of people, often hostile, at board meetings who try to disrupt the meeting and bring business to a grinding halt. Attacking the process and looking for weak spots (or weak people) can be effective.

There may be ballot initiatives demanding some action: attacks on funding, recall campaigns of elected officials, etc. There may be delaying tactics and attempts to hold up bond issues for school or library funding or construction. You will often hear ALA, its policies, and librarians in general attacked verbally. Often the information about ALA is not correct.

Librarians may find themselves pitted against other librarians in other libraries or buildings who have not purchased the materials in question. Challengers often try to promote hostility between parents and schools and between patrons and libraries, or will claim that they speak for everybody in a community.

There is a whole group of tactics that are not illegal but are recognized as part of the legitimate democratic process. These are sometimes called "guerrilla tactics." They include using the system to check out a book and never returning it. Lies about ALA and its policies and the outcome of Supreme Court cases, such as *Pico,* may seem to work for a while until challenged by a librarian. Personal attacks with innuendo and smear campaigns are popular as censorship challenges heat up. Librarians may also receive anonymous letters.

Many librarians and board members who have lived through long, drawn-out, and hostile challenges report that they are often threatened. Their staff or family may also be threatened. Vandalism, against the book or against people, may be common. Challengers may use intimidating tactics aimed at board members and library staff (at testimony, in letters) and personal attacks—in writing, oral, physical. Putting mail in mail boxes without postage is against federal law. Some librarians report bomb threats to their homes or libraries. These tactics (which are often used) definitely fall into the category of unacceptable and often illegal. Consult your local police if any of these things are happening during a challenge in your community.

When guerrilla and illegal tactics are used, the tenor of a censorship challenge changes. When individuals begin to use tactics that are outside of the legal and democratic process, it is appropriate to talk with local police. It is also OK to rethink your bottom line when threatened and scared. For some librarians there will be no change; others may back out of being actively involved.

CARRYING ON

The last board member has voted—you are either elated or in the dumps. This won't be the first or the last censorship battle you ever face. You may have gathered piles of documents and other useful information. Think of all the people who have helped during the challenge. The first item on the to-do list is to write thank-you notes to everybody who helped you in any way during the censorship challenge. The second item, which is for the long-range goals list, is to think about ways you can make a broader contribution to intellectual freedom. Serving on your state association's intellectual freedom committee, making sure that Banned Books Week is celebrated in your community, and giving workshops and in-service programs for colleagues are just a few of the ways you can participate professionally. Don't let this be the end of your involvement with intellectual freedom.

CUYAHOGA COUNTY PUBLIC LIBRARY
2111 Snow Road • Parma, Ohio 44134–2792 • (216) 398–1800 FAX (216) 398–6104

July 23, 1993

The board and administration of Cuyahoga County Public Library have read, discussed and considered your letter of June 22, 1993. We take seriously all questions and criticisms about the Library's policies and procedures.

The Board of Trustees continues to support the American Library Association's "Freedom to Read" statement. This statement specifically provides that "it is in the public interest for publishers and librarians to make available the widest diversity of views and expressions, including those which are unorthodox or unpopular with the majority." It goes on to state that, "Publishers, librarians and booksellers do not need to endorse every idea or presentation contained in the books they make available. It would conflict with the public interest for them to establish their own political, moral or aesthetic views as a standard for determining what books should be published or circulated."

Libraries are forums for information and ideas. The public library provides alternatives for people to make choices. All libraries contain some printed and audiovisual materials which some parents might find inappropriate for their children. We maintain that libraries cannot act *in loco parentis.* Therefore, we encourage parents to exercise their responsibilities to guide and monitor what their children read and view. Denying access to minors would be in disagreement with what the free public library stands for in American society. That is, access to all persons, regardless of origin, age, background, or views.

We recognize that Madonna's book contains sexually explicit material that may be offensive to some members of the community. Your letter makes reference to The State of Ohio Revised Code, Section 2907.31. Under "C" of this section, it states that, "It is an affirmative defense to a charge under this section, involving material or a performance which is obscene or harmful to juveniles, that such material or performance was furnished or presented for a bona fide medical, scientific, educational, governmental, judicial, or other proper purpose, by a physician, psychologist, sociologist, scientist, teacher, librarian, clergyman, prosecutor, judge, or other proper person."

The "Freedom to Read" statement also provides that "it is the responsibility of publishers and librarians as guardians of the peoples' freedom to read to contest encroachments upon that freedom by individuals or groups seeking to impose their own standards or tastes upon the community at large."

We appreciate every opportunity to reinforce our position on this matter so that people have a clearer understanding of the public library's role in society. Thank you for taking the time to write.

Very truly yours,

Claudya B. Muller, Executive Director

Reprinted with permission of the Cuyahoga County Public Library.

REFERENCES

American Association of School Librarians. "Position Statement on: The Role of the School Library Media Program." Chicago: American Library Association, 1990.

American Library Association, Office for Intellectual Freedom. "A Guide to Working with the Media." Chicago: American Library Association, n.d.

Doyle, Robert P. *Banned Books Resource Guide.* Chicago: American Library Association, 1994.

Hopkins, Dianne McAfee. "Factors Influencing the Outcome of Library Media Center Challenges at the Secondary Level." *School Library Media Quarterly,* (Summer 1990).

Intellectual Freedom Manual. Compiled by June Pinnell Stephens for the Alaska Library Association, Intellectual Freedom Committee. Juneau, AK: Alaska State Library, Alaska Department of Education, 1985.

Krug, Judith F., and Anne Penway. "Public Library Censorship" in *How to Win: A Practical Guide for Defeating the Radical Right in Your Community.* [Comp. by] Radical Right Task Force, National Jewish Democratic Council. Washington, DC: The Council, 1994.

9 TRENDS AND ISSUES IN INTELLECTUAL FREEDOM

This chapter progresses from a historical review of censorship and libraries to censorship today and to four areas that are certain to affect intellectual freedom in the coming decade. Statistics from People for the American Way and the ALA Office for Intellectual Freedom are presented and discussed. The increasingly aggressive nature of organized pressure groups and their effect on today's library are examined.

As with any facet of contemporary life, today's intellectual freedom issues are influenced by public opinion, media coverage of controversies, information technology, and instant communication that enables disparate people and groups to quickly coalesce into formidable pressure groups. The convergence of these separate phenomena has significantly increased the number, scope, and sophistication of formal reconsideration requests filed in libraries.

HISTORICAL VIEW

Frances M. Jones provides a wonderful history of censorship in her book *Defusing Censorship*. She tells us that as early as A.D. 95, Christians were prohibited from reading certain works by the Apostolic Constitution, and 200 years later writers of works considered heretical were sentenced to death. With the advent of printed books, efforts to suppress publication grew. For example, by 1586, books printed in England had to have the prior approval of either the Archbishop of Canterbury or the Bishop of London. The British government subsequently tried to control publishing both by requiring government licensing before publication and by granting a monopoly on printing to one company. In 1644, John Milton responded to one government action with *Areopagitica* in which, among other points, he observes that (as paraphrased by Jones), "If books were prohibited because of some error in them, the truth in them would also be lost" (Jones 1983, #3). Milton's assertion is an early statement of the distinction between censorship and selection—censorship being the suppression of materials because of some objection and selection being a positive action based on some good quality.

Events of the seventeenth and eighteenth centuries such as rebellion against colonialism and slavery, increasing acceptance of individual liberties, and growing literacy rates created an atmosphere that helped foster the Declaration of Independence, the U.S. Constitution, and the Bill of Rights. In adopting the First Amendment, Jones says, our "nation's founders expressed their collective belief in the dignity of each human and in the right of each citizen to pursue truth unaided and unimpeded by the state" (Jones 1983, 3). Censorship in the 1800s dealt less with religious and political matters and more with personal morals and obscenity.

Judith Krug and James A. Harvey report that the American Library Association first "indicated its future approach to censorship when the ALA Executive Board [in 1929] studied a proposed federal tariff bill and opposed prohibition of importing materials 'advocating or urging treason, insurrection, or forcible resistance to any law of the U.S. . . . or any obscene book, paper, etc.'" (Krug 1992, xv). The ALA Executive Board's rationale for this action included the objection that such a prohibition would be "a reflection upon the intelligence of the American people by implying that they are so stupid and untrustworthy that they cannot read about revolutions without becoming revolutionaries" (Krug 1992, xv). This specific objection, one of five the Executive Board cited, is particularly noteworthy because it resounds again and again throughout almost every challenge to library materials.

In 1934, ALA made its first formal protest against the banning of a specific publication, *You and Machines*. During that same decade, the Association's basic intellectual freedom position became clear when John Steinbeck's *The Grapes of Wrath* became the target of censors around the country and was actually banned in libraries from New Jersey to California. Some challenges were based on the perceived immorality of the work, others on the social views advanced by the author. These widespread challenges culminated in ALA's original adoption of the Library's Bill of Rights in 1939 (later called the Library Bill of Rights). Various amendments were made through the years codifying individuals' rights to use libraries regardless of race, religion, national origin, or political views (1961) and age (1967) (Krug 1992, xv–xvii).

In understanding the history of intellectual freedom and libraries, it is important to realize that ALA's actions both paralleled and reflected activities in America's libraries. Librarians didn't come to ALA conferences and adopt the Library Bill of Rights just because they wanted something to do in 1939. They did this because day in and day out, materials were being challenged in libraries where they worked. When these same librarians came to an ALA conference, they wanted their professional association to act so that all librarians spoke with a clear and unified voice. Our predecessors saw that it was essential that librarians serving communities of all sizes have a national body of policy to turn for guidance and from which they could adapt policies governing the operation of their own libraries. This guidance and policy were needed to respond to efforts to restrict access to information.

Librarians today owe a great debt to ALA for its work in this area because there has been no shortage of censorship attempts in the past few decades. In 1972, America's courts considered their first case involving whether a school board could remove books from a school library (*President's Council, District 25* v. *Community School Board No. 25* [New York City]). Some members of the community asked the school board to remove Piri Thomas's *Down These Mean Streets* from a junior high school library because they were offended by its language and sexual content. Henry Reichman, in *Censorship and Selection: Issues and Answers for Schools,* says that in upholding the book's removal, the U.S. Court of Appeals for the Second Circuit "declared that someone has to bear responsibility for book selection, and since school boards are statutorily empowered to operate the schools and prescribe the curriculum, the board is the appropriate body" (Reichman 1993, 148). The rights of school boards were reaffirmed in 1979–1980 when federal courts dismissed complaints in Vermont about the removal of two books (*The Wanderer* and *Dog Day Afternoon*) from Vergness Union High School Library, the imposition of a freeze on new library acquisitions, and the board's policy of screening all new major acquisitions. Again, Reichman tells us, "The court held that school boards have final authority in such matters and that the restrictions did not violate the constitutional rights of students or librarians." This latter case foretells coming trends in censorship because those seeking to restrict access extended their reach from two specific titles to the entire selection and acquisition process; the board also extended its reach from policy purview into the library's operations.

In 1982, the U.S. Supreme Court addressed the issue of books in the school library in a landmark case, *Pico* v. *Board of Education, Island Trees Union Free School District No. 26* (usually referred to as *Pico*). In September 1975, a politically conservative organization informed three school board members that nine books—including *Slaughterhouse Five, Best Short Stories of Negro Writers,* and *Go Ask Alice*—were objectionable. The following year, the board gave an "unofficial direction" that these books be removed from the district's libraries so that they could read them. When their action attracted press attention, the three board members issued a press release describing the books as "anti-American, anti-Christian, anti-Semitic, and just plain filthy." Although a board committee appointed by the board made less restrictive recommendations, the board ordered that eight of the nine books be removed without explaining its action. A group of students filed a challenge to the board's actions and, in a 5–4 decision, the Supreme Court upheld the students' challenge (Reichman 1993, 152–53).

Pico can be seen as setting the stage for today's censorship environment because it involved a politically savvy approach by a conservative organization to selected members of a school board. Today, we see representatives of organized groups simultaneously filing multiple challenges to titles. These groups also seek to get their representatives elected and appointed to school and public library boards. It is important to understand the ways in which these groups work, the types of materials they and individuals file objections to, and the explosive growth in the numbers of challenges actually filed.

CENSORSHIP TODAY

Unfortunately, most libraries don't report censorship attempts to ALA, so we really don't know the true extent of challenges filed. Consider the relationship between the number of attempts reported in one state, Colorado, for an idea of the magnitude of the censors' threat to library collections. In 1993 at least 337 challenges to materials were made in Colorado's public libraries alone. Julie Boucher, associate director of the Colorado State Library and Adult Education Office's Library Research Service, reports that "while nine out of ten reporting libraries indicated they would notify governing boards [of a challenge], less than one out of ten would notify CLA [the Colorado Library Association] or ALA" (Boucher 1994, 1). What this tells us is that the number of challenges reported to ALA is just a fraction of the number actually occurring each year in libraries across the nation. For example, ALA recorded 760 challenges in 1994 (American Library Association 1995b, 1). Knowing that 337 challenges were filed in Colorado public libraries alone in 1993, and knowing that half of all challenges across the nation didn't happen in Colorado, it's obvious that there is drastic underreporting going on. Notifying ALA's

Office for Intellectual Freedom whenever there is a challenge to library materials will help ALA track trends as well as provide you with invaluable support, assistance, and advice.

Figure 9-1 summarizes key information (except for the basis for the complaint, which is covered later) about the 760 challenges that were reported to ALA in 1994. Notice that schools account for 521 (or 68.5 percent) of the year's challenges. Notice too that 491 (64.6 percent) of these were filed by parents (466) or teachers (25). Thus, the majority of challenges filed had, in some way, shape, or form, the motivation to shield children or young people from materials the challenger believed was in some way harmful to them. Librarians and other educators have learned, though, that most challenges are not simply a case of parents accidentally coming across a book or other material that they find offensive.

FIGURE 9–1 Key points (except for grounds) about challenges reported to ALA's Office for Intellectual Freedom in 1994 (American Library Association 1995b, 1).

Number of challenges: 760

What was challenged:		
	639	Books
	25	Magazines
	14	Textbooks
	13	Student publications
	12	Videos
	11	Artworks
	46	Others (Pamphlets, films, exhibits, etc.)

Who initiated the challenges

Individuals		
	466	Parents
	124	Patrons
	55	Administrators
	25	Teachers
	18	Board members
	18	Clergy

Groups		
	24	Pressure groups
	13	Religious organizations
	3	Government organizations
	3	Other groups

Type of institution challenged		
	319	School libraries
	206	Public libraries
	202	School (other than the school's library)
	4	Academic libraries
	1	Prison library
	13	Other institution

People for the American Way, for instance, reported in the fall of 1994 that "large numbers of right-wing political organizations, along with their local activist allies, have been waging a comprehensive, highly organized campaign to challenge library books, classroom materials and a broad range of school programs and reforms" (Witt 1994, 1). Most people filing challenges to school materials are not just seeking to "protect" or "shield" *their* children from material they find offensive either. In fact, of the 375 incidents documented by People for the American Way during the 1993–94 school year, 62 (or 16.5 percent) involved demands that the materials be kept from all students. These challenged materials spanned the curriculum: literature anthologies, biology textbooks, library books and magazines, titles on summer reading lists, student plays, and the sex education curriculum. The originators of these challenges are often not simply outraged parents acting in isolation. People for the American Way reported that "Religious Right political groups led the [censorship] charge, lending technical, legal, or even financial support in 22 percent of all documented incidents. Further, in an additional 14 percent of the challenges, targets, strategies, and rhetoric appeared to be inspired by these groups" (Witt 1994, 1).

The largest and most active of these groups are Citizens for Excellence in Education, Focus on the Family, the Eagle Forum, Concerned Women for America, the American Family Association, the Rutherford Institute, Traditional Values Coalition, and the National Parents Commission. According to People for the American Way, these groups seek to "Christianize" American society by using direct mail, newsletters, and extensive grassroots mobilization strategies "to ignite attacks on school programs and library materials that do not fit their sectarian ideology" (People for the American Way 1994, 6).

People for the American Way has also identified a composite model of censorship campaigns these groups use. Librarians should familiarize themselves with this model, reprinted in figure 9-2, so that they can distinguish between an organized pressure campaign and a complaint brought by an individual parent, teacher, or patron.

It always helps to understand why people or groups act as they do. By achieving such an understanding of the motives underlying someone's behaviors, we can better respond to their actions. Library Director James LaRue has developed a conceptual framework presenting what he calls the premises of democracy (upholding people's right to read and know) and the premises of censorship (which underlie arguments used to restrict access) (LaRue 1994). This framework can assist us in understanding both

---

FIGURE 9–2   Composite Model of a Religious Right Censorship Campaign (People for the American Way 1994, 6).

- A local group distributes materials in churches and throughout the community to mobilize opposition to a particular book or program;
- The group demands the book or program be removed, usually appealing directly to the school board;
- Group members use intense lobbying and often threats of legal action to pressure the board;
- The group often responds to school board rejection of their demands with costly lawsuits, school board recall campaigns, or attempts to defeat school tax levies;
- Religious Right groups often sponsor candidates to run for local school boards and, once elected, to carry out their agenda.

---

how librarians and First Amendment supporters think (and why we act as we do) and, perhaps more importantly, why organized groups and concerned individuals find libraries' provision of some materials offensive and are sufficiently motivated to file formal complaints.

LaRue's premises effectively contrast the arguments espoused by those who seek to censor with the counterpoints used by those

Premises of democracy	Premises of censorship
• Literacy is better than illiteracy • Knowledge is better than ignorance • Tolerance is better than intolerance	• The book made me do it • It's a conspiracy • Library materials should reflect community standards • Community standards are inherently correct • Library materials should present only positive role models

who defend free and open access to library materials. Whereas the organized right uses blanket arguments that essentially conclude that if young adults read about drugs and gay sex, they'll become gay drug users (LaRue's premise that "the book made me do it"), librarians believe that if young adults read realistic fiction and accurate nonfiction materials about drugs and sex, they will be better informed to make healthy life choices (LaRue's premise that "knowledge is better than ignorance"). It is from these very different premises (or perspectives) that would-be censors and librarians view the same materials. Challengers encounter a book or a video and see it as a threat to readers, as potentially harmful to a child's soul or mind as an identified, visible virus would be to the child's body.

To recap, we know that: (1) most censorship attempts involve the shielding of minors from materials and (2) approximately 36 percent of these are in some way assisted or inspired by organized pressure groups. What types of materials are these individuals and groups targeting?

ALA's Office for Intellectual Freedom reported that the most challenged book in 1994 was *Daddy's Roommate* by Michael Willhoite. That title had that same distinction in 1993. (See chapter 7 for a detailed case study of a *Daddy's Roommate* challenge). *Heather Has Two Mommies* (by Leslea Newman) and *Scary Stories to Tell in the Dark* (by Alvin Schwartz) tied for the second most challenged title in 1994 (American Library Association 1995a, 1). Figure 9-3 displays the most challenged books for the period September 1, 1990–December 31, 1994 according to ALA's Office for Intellectual Freedom.

FIGURE 9–3   The ten titles most frequently challenged in libraries between September 1, 1990 and December 31, 1994 according to the American Library Association Office for Intellectual Freedom's database. (American Library Association 1995a, 1)

Rank	Title	Author	No. of Challenges
1	Daddy's Roommate	Michael Willhoite	80
2	Impressions Reading Series	Harcourt Brace Jovanovich	44
3	More Scary Stories to Tell in the Dark	Alvin Schwartz	33
4	Heather Has Two Mommies	Leslea Newman	29
4	Scary Stories to Tell in the Dark	Alvin Schwartz	29
5	Bridge to Terabithia	Katherine Patterson	26
6	Sex	Madonna	25
7	Forever	Judy Blume	21
8	The Adventures of Huckleberry Finn	Mark Twain	20
8	Of Mice and Men	John Steinbeck	20

Other than these most-challenged titles, what kinds of materials evoke this strong reaction from individuals and organized groups?

The OIF classifies the grounds used to challenge library material into four categories: cultural, sexual, values, or social issues. Challenges filed in 1994 broke down as follows:

Cultural (9%)		Sexual (35%)		Values (35%)		Social Issues (21%)	
Anti-ethnic	7	Homosexuality	91	Anti-family	19	Abortion	3
Insensitivity	10	Nudity	40	Offensive language	155	Drugs	19
Racism	17	Sex education	37	Political view	12	Occult/Satan	107
Sexism	10	Sexually explicit	183	Religious view	55	Violence	78
Other	49			Unsuited to age	104	Suicide	5

Because challengers may cite multiple grounds for their objections to library materials, the total number of grounds reported exceeds 760 (the number of challenges reported to ALA OIF in 1994). These reasons were remarkably similar to the top reasons cited for challenges to materials in Australian school libraries. According to a presentation made by Ken Dillon at the Canadian Library Association's 1994 conference, the top grounds cited for challenges in Australia were: morality (16 percent), obscenity (14 percent), profanity (11 percent), witchcraft (9 percent), violence (8 percent), human reproduction (8 percent), immaturity (7 percent), religion (except for evolution) (7 percent), defiance of authority (5 percent), and nudity (5 percent) (Moore 1994, 28). This comparison shows that the reasons for challenges are remarkably similar across the world.

Further information about current challenges can be gleaned from Colorado's analysis of 1993 public library challenges: nine out of ten challenged titles had copyright dates of 1985 or later, two-thirds of challenged titles were fiction, and half of all challenged titles were children's or young adult materials (Boucher 1994, 1).

DEVELOPING TRENDS AND THE FUTURE

Many complainants now seek to go beyond challenging specific titles and aggressively press for fundamental reforms in the ways libraries operate. Four areas of debate involving intellectual freedom issues are of paramount concern to librarians in the latter half of this decade and will profoundly affect libraries' ability to serve their communities' total spectrum well into the twenty-first century. These are: youth access to library resources, the place of religious materials in library collections, gay and lesbian materials, and multiculturalism. Be assured that these issues will not just go away if they are "kept quiet so everybody's happy"; instead, their impact will grow stronger. By recognizing the fundamental and overarching importance of these issues, librarians can proactively rethink their policies and procedures, develop positive public relations tools educating users and others about their policies, and appropriately develop their collections to reflect changing community demographics and interests.

YOUTH ACCESS

The late 1980s and early 1990s brought a rash of controversies involving youth access to library resources to the public arena. Library acquisition of Madonna's *Sex* probably got as much press coverage as any library issue in history. Many of the more notable controversies, particularly in terms of media coverage, took place in the Pacific Northwest. The Fort Vancouver (Washington) Regional Library sponsored a forum in 1993 to discuss these issues and patrons recommended many changes in library policy at the forum. Changes considered by the library's Policy Committee included such fundamental issues as:

- restricting a minor's circulation privileges to only juvenile materials at the parent's request;
- issuing multiple "family cards" so that parents could see what their children had checked out;
- using taxpayer money to buy only materials that met the interests of a majority in the community;
- establishing a selection and/or materials review committee with citizen members;
- keeping sensitive materials on a closed shelf;
- putting certain sexually explicit and "alternative lifestyle materials" in the headquarters building with access through the computer reserve system only;
- apprising parents of newly acquired sensitive materials; and
- rating and labeling books in a fashion similar to that used for movies.

As the board's Policy Committee discussed these issues, its goal was to help families use the library in a manner they found acceptable without infringing on the rights of other families. Following hearings and over 200 hours of deliberation, the Policy Committee and the library board voted not to adopt any of the changes that involved parental control. It concluded that:

Fort Vancouver Regional Library has traditionally upheld the private rights of everyone to read what they choose, regardless of their age. While the Library has helped parents guide the selection choices of their own minor children, it had remained completely neutral in the process. Each of the options would change that traditional neutral role of the Library. If any of the options are adopted, the Library, a governmental agency, would be assisting parents in enforcing their own family rules and values (Fort Vancouver [Washington] Regional Library 1993).

The Fort Vancouver situation, when it was over, successfully upheld both the traditional values of libraries and the rights of citizens in the community to access information. It also reaffirmed parents' rights and responsibilities to monitor the reading choices of their own children—but only their own children. Librarians facing similar controversies or wishing to prepare for such controversies are referred to the library's full report for its well-reasoned decisions and policy analyses.

THE IMPORTANCE OF RELIGIOUS MATERIALS

Because public and school libraries serve the total spectrum of their community and because diversity in collection development encompasses religious diversity, librarians have a responsibility to provide books and other media that reflect religious values. This means selecting novels that feature Christian characters, inspirational fiction, books of prayers for various occasions, etc. Just as we argue that we must buy books with gay characters because some members of the community are gay, we have an obligation to provide books in which religious readers can see people like them treated in a positive light.

It is important today and will be increasingly important in the years to come that religious print and nonprint materials be found in the children's, young adult, and adult collections. Consider, for example, the positive value of the following hypothetical encounter. A Christian parent comes into the library looking for some books to take home to her young son. She browses carefully through several novels and then comes to the children's librarian and says that none of them are appropriate. When asked why, she responds that they don't reflect her values. If the library's collection included a good selection of inspirational fiction intended for children of her son's age, the librarian could then end the encounter happily. If, however (as is too often the case), the collection includes little or no inspirational fiction, the parent could quite rightfully argue that the collection is biased.

Review media such as *School Library Journal, Booklist,* and *Library Journal* increasingly include bibliographies and special features reviewing fiction and nonfiction religious materials. Library conferences also include programs devoted to this topic and these sometimes provide handouts of retrospective bibliographies and listings of publishers and suppliers of religious materials. Local religious bookstores are yet another source of both advice and materials. Asking store owners for advice will further both public relations and collection development. Librarians are strongly encouraged to seek these review sources out and regularly include materials of religious interest in collections.

GAY AND LESBIAN MATERIALS

This one's not going away, and there's no way to make controversies over providing information and materials of interest to gay citizens a pleasant encounter for librarians, gay patrons, or complainants. LaRue's premises about censorship and democracy referred to earlier in this chapter underlie the reasons for this ongoing discordance. Another reason is that many homophobic people don't acknowledge the existence of "normal-looking" gay people. One study recently showed that even other gay people are wrong as often as right in correctly guessing the sexual orientation of others. As Cal Gough and Ellen Greenblatt observed in their article "Services to Gay and Lesbian Patrons: Examining the Myths," "For all you know, the young Asian female, child in tow, standing in front of your reference desk . . . might also be left-handed, a jogger, a good cook, and a lesbian" (Gough 1992, 60).

Very heated public controversy and many people's inherent uncomfortableness in dealing with gay and lesbian issues converge to make this developing trend the most threatening one for librarians. ALA, in adopting an interpretation of the Library Bill of Rights dealing with equal access regardless of gender or sexual orientation (reprinted in Appendix A), has provided librarians with policy on which to draw for proactively preparing for challenges and to which to refer people when they ask, "But why does this stuff have to be in 'our' library?" Another way to deal with complaints about gay-positive materials in libraries is to provide an alternative viewpoint as well. Diversity in collection development calls for representing all points of view; that homosexuality can be "cured" is certainly one point of view. And, regardless of your personal feelings about homosexuality or gay people, adding something to the collection is much better than removing materials or restricting access.

MULTICULTURALISM

With historical minorities now comprising the majority of populations in an increasing number of areas within the U.S., librarians have an affirmative obligation in developing both library services and library collections to serve diverse populations. This obligation requires us to rethink the way we interact with people, the languages we speak, the languages we collect materials in, the signs on our doors and our shelves, and the ethnicity of characters in our books, videos, and interactive fiction.

As they have with religious materials, review media, library literature, and continuing education events such as conferences and workshops increasingly include segments devoted to multicultural services. By taking a proactive approach to ensuring that the library's collections and services meet the needs of the community's members and that all people find what they need when they come to the library, librarians can prevent complaints and better serve their communities.

Librarians will increasingly need to be prepared to justify the inclusiveness of their collections and sources when confronted with intolerance. This includes being prepared to continue purchasing materials in languages used in the community as the "English Only" movement grows. The interpretation of the Library Bill of Rights dealing with "Diversity in Collection Development" and "Access to Resources and Services in the School Library Media Program" (especially the fourth paragraph) are strong resources for making this argument. Both are reprinted in Appendix A.

PREPARING FOR THE FUTURE

Current policy and practice in both school and public libraries come from a long-standing and well-documented legal and philosophical tradition of serving all community members. This tradition and practice is being challenged all over our country as it never has before. These challenges are well organized, well funded, and well documented. Librarians should be aware of how pressure groups organize locally and operate so that they can obtain the necessary help and advice to defend the rights of citizens in their communities.

Four trends that began in the late 1980s and early 1990s and will continue to strongly affect intellectual freedom in libraries well into the twenty-first century are youth access issues, religious materials, gay materials, and multicultural materials and services. A fifth major trend, access to electronic resources, has emerged in 1995 and is discussed both in chapter 3 on concerns specific to public libraries (in regard to library fees) and in chapter 5 on threats to intellectual freedom on the information superhighway.

REFERENCES

American Library Association, Office for Intellectual Freedom. "*Daddy's Rommate* Most Challenged Book of 1994." *Intellectual Freedom Action News* (January 1995), 1.

American Library Association, Office for Intellectual Freedom. "OIF Censorship Database, Summary of Challenges, January 1, 1994-December 31, 1994." Unpublished, 1995.

Boucher, Julie. "Censorship in Colorado Public Libraries 1993." *Fast Facts* no. 90 (November 1, 1994).

Fort Vancouver [Washington] Regional Library. *Policy on Children's Access to Library Materials: 1993.* Vancouver, WA: Fort Vancouver Regional Library, 1993.

Gough, Cal, and Ellen Greenblatt. "Services to Gay and Lesbian Patrons: Examining the Myths." *Library Journal* (January 1992).

Jones, Frances M. *Defusing Censorship: The Librarian's Guide to Handling Censorship Conflicts.* Phoenix, AZ: Oryx Press, 1983.

Krug, Judith, and James A. Harvey. "ALA and Intellectual Freedom: A Historical Overview" in *Intellectual Freedom Manual*, 4th ed. Chicago: American Library Association, 1992.

LaRue, James. "Reading with the Enemy." *Wilson Library Bulletin* (January 1994), 43–44.

Moore, Mary J. "Censorship and School Libraries in Australia and Canada." *Feliciter*, (September 1994).

People for the American Way. *An Activist's Guide to Protecting the Freedom to Learn.* Washington, DC: People for the American Way, 1994.

Reichman, Henry. *Censorship and Selection: Issues and Answers for Schools.* Chicago: American Library Association, 1993.

Witt, Virginia. "School Censorship Attempts Hit Twelve-Year High." *People for the American Way News*, 1, no. 1 (Fall 1994), 1.

10 CONCLUSION

This chapter takes all the individual pieces that must come together in order to protect the right to read and looks at how they came together in two specific library settings.

That intellectual freedom is a foundation essential for democracy to thrive has been a common thread throughout this book. Protecting the right to read requires convincing administrators (whether school or municipal government), parents, and citizens in general that any threat to the right to read, listen, or view opens the door to a future threat to their own rights. The old story "first they came for the Jews, but I wasn't a Jew, so I didn't say anything; then they came for the Communists, but I wasn't a Communist, so I didn't say anything; and then when they came for me, there was nobody left to speak for me" is just as applicable to the insidious nature of censorship as it is to the rampant spread of nationalistic paranoia in Nazi Germany. If people think it's OK to censor *Daddy's Roommate* because they want to protect children from the idea of gayness, who's to say that it's not OK to censor *The Joy of Sex* because it might make college students horny, or *The Merchant of Venice* because it might incite anti-Semitism in today's hate-radio filled environment?

Librarians have a special responsibility in maintaining the First Amendment foundation of democracy. As chapter 1 pointed out, our core professional documents, the ALA Code of Ethics and the Library Bill of Rights, require us to resist any effort by groups or individuals to censor library materials. The Library Bill of Rights also calls for libraries to cooperate with other groups that resist the abridgment of free expression and free access to ideas. As the chapter on the Internet made clear, our responsibilities in this area become both broader and more complex as the Internet grows in popularity and sophistication.

In acknowledging that librarians have major responsibilities in these areas, this book has also made clear that no librarian need ever be alone in developing policies and procedures or when the censor knocks at his or her library's door or pings his or her Web site. A wealth of print, electronic, and human resources stand ready to provide assistance of all types.

Our most important two pieces of advice are: (1) every library should have and use up-to-date, clear, board-approved policies and procedures governing selection and access policies and (2) every librarian should be aware of and communicate those policies to any patron, teacher, or citizen who has a concern about the library or any specific title or titles in it. An informal conversation in which the librarian listens to a person who has a complaint about a title and calmly talks about the library's duty to serve *all* segments of the community and an understanding that the library cannot act *in loco parentis* has prevented many more censorship challenges than have ever been filed.

The old joke that polite dinner conversation avoids politics and religion goes right to the heart of people's convictions about what should and what should not be in a library. Many conservative religious people sincerely don't want their tax dollars used on or their children to have access to books containing sex, profanity, or the occult. Likewise, many vocal liberal citizens may find books that advocate school prayer, home schooling, or restorative therapies for homosexuals to be a less-than-wise investment of their hard-earned tax dollars. As Mary K. Chelton has said on many occasions, "Your library should have something to offend everyone." This book's section on selection policies, collection development, and the interpretation of the Library Bill of Rights dealing with diversity in library collections can be of great help to librarians struggling with these issues or caught between competing community pressure groups.

As the case study chapter brought to life, a formal challenge can result in incredible publicity and divisive, emotional public debate involving people's most closely held beliefs. For example, a recent censorship incident involving the Lincolnwood (Illinois) Public Library mirrored today's headlines. As reported in the *Newsletter on Intellectual Freedom*, a local citizen called Alex Dragnich's *Serbs and Croats* "a damn lie" and felt that it "should not be in any library because [it's] written with one only purpose and that is to defame" ("Success Stories" 1995, 53). He said that book was pro-Serbian and anti-Croatian. When the citizen, Vladimir Baisch,

> who works for the Croatian Cultural Council in Chicago, returned the Dragnich book . . . it was covered with written comments. Librarians told him he would have to pay for it, but, according to a police report on the incident, he grew abusive and hinted that he and other Croatians would burn down the library if the book were not taken off the shelves. Baisch later paid for the volume and no charges were filed.

Cynthia Josephs, the library's director, conferred with Baisch and ordered three books that he recommended. Several Serbians attended a board meeting after news about Baisch's complaint was aired on a Serbian radio station. The *Newsletter* reported that a Serbian spokesperson said that the solution was acceptable if the Dragnich book and several others remained in the library. The board's president, Ben Siegel, said, "The library does not have political opinions. We try to buy the best possible books as we see them to enable people to form their own opinions."

The Croatian/Serbian conflict over perspectives available in the library mirrors in many ways the Juneau, Alaska, conflict over the definition of "family" presented in *Daddy's Roommate*. Likewise, Siegel's summation of what the library does and does not stand for mirrors the Juneau school board's determination to resist bigotry no matter what form it takes and to serve all parts of the community.

Censorship, whether it takes the form of a formal challenge, political pressure from administrators or board members, peer pressure from colleagues, threats of physical violence, or people simply checking out or stealing books they object to, is scary and costly. The best way to prevent it is to be prepared, know where to get help if you need it, and stay calm.

While censorship challenges are certainly best avoided by following these steps, if they do occur, librarians are encouraged to get help and to try to use the incident to provide an opportunity for:

- Paving the way for community acceptance and appreciation of a diverse collection;
- Providing a real-life laboratory for demonstrating the value and importance of the First Amendment;
- Affirming the value of the library as a public forum for exchanging ideas and information; and
- Helping the community face its prejudices and affirm its tolerance.

In closing, consider the story of Lenore Bright, director of Sisson Memorial Library in Pagosa Springs, Colorado, and her first censorship encounter. She had a patron whom she describes as having a pathological disorder and who had been kicked out of several churches because he would create a disturbance whenever he disagreed with a sermon. Bright says that he would bring his preschool-age son to the library for hours every day but would not allow the child "to read or look at any anthropomorphic books because he considered talking animals to be the work of the devil" (Bright 1993, 15). Further, the child couldn't listen to story hours or participate in any of the children's activities. The father would make critical comments about various books but never created a problem until Bright purchased two books on the pros and cons of euthanasia.

When the patron discovered Doris Protwook's *Commonsense Suicide* on the new book shelf, Bright reports, "he became irrational. He accosted my staff and began screaming and demanding they remove the book. They were afraid because his verbal abuse bordered on actual physical violence." Bright says that she was not in the library at this time and that a staff member gave him a reconsideration form and told him to discuss the book with her. He photocopied pages from the book, distributed them to church leaders, stopped people on the street, and went into local stores to try to get people angered about the book.

Bright explains that she had selection and reconsideration policies in place, including a standing committee to advise the board on any request to remove material. When the patron returned the book to her, she told him about the committee, that they would read the book, and make a decision. Bright says, "He became violent again and I warned him that if he continued to threaten me or the staff, I would get a restraining order and he would not be allowed to come in the library any more. As I said this, I must admit I was envisioning all of the crazed killers one reads about who come back with their automatic weapons to wipe out their perceived enemies." She goes on to say that he calmed down, they discussed his objections, and that he truly believed that the book would cause community teens to commit suicide. This last point echoes numerous references throughout this book that complainants often sincerely believe that material in the library can do serious harm. The patron wrote an impassioned plea to the reconsideration committee. Bright says that "Judith Krug from ALA sent us reviews of the book, and gave us all kinds of support. Nancy Knepel, current High Plains System Director, also helped with reviews and strong moral support when we needed it most. The process worked well, it was an educational experience destined to prepare us for any future encounters." The incident concluded with the committee advising the board to keep the book (Bright 1993, 15).

Bright's story is a fitting conclusion to *Protecting the Right to Read: A How-To-Do-It Manual for School and Public Librarians* because it shows that success depends on being prepared and getting help from both ALA and your local support system when a challenge first comes up.

By understanding the role of the library, developing and communicating policies and procedures, following those procedures, and knowing where to get help when it is needed, all librarians can help protect people's rights to access words, images, and sound in all formats.

REFERENCES

Bright, Lenore. "Censorship in a Small Town." *Colorado Libraries* (Summer 1993), 15.

"Success Stories: Lincolnwood, Illinois." *Newsletter on Intellectual Freedom* 44, no. 2 (March 1995), 53.

APPENDIX A:

INTERPRETATIONS OF THE LIBRARY BILL OF RIGHTS AND ASSOCIATED GUIDELINES

The documents reprinted here with the gracious permission of the American Library Association represent the core intellectual freedom statements that guide decisions made by librarians across the country every day. They are included here in the hope they will be adopted by even more governing boards, incorporated into additional library policy manuals, and guide even more decisions affecting users' access to information on a daily basis. The Library Bill of Rights itself appears on page 7.

CONTENTS OF THIS APPENDIX

ACCESS FOR CHILDREN AND YOUNG PEOPLE TO VIDEOTAPES AND OTHER NONPRINT FORMATS

An Interpretation of the Library Bill of Rights

Library collections of videotapes, motion pictures, and other nonprint formats raise a number of intellectual freedom issues, especially regarding minors.

The interests of young people, like those of adults, are not limited by subject, theme, or level of sophistication. Librarians have a responsibility to ensure young people have access to materials and services that reflect diversity sufficient to meet their needs.

To guide librarians and others in resolving these issues, the American Library Association provides the following guidelines.

Article V of the LIBRARY BILL OF RIGHTS says, "A person's right to use a library should not be denied or abridged because of origin, age, background, or views."

ALA's FREE ACCESS TO LIBRARIES FOR MINORS: An Interpretation of the LIBRARY BILL OF RIGHTS states:

> The "right to use a library" includes free access to, and unrestricted use of, all the services, materials, and facilities the library has to offer. Every restriction on access to, and use of, library resources, based solely on the chronological age, educational level, or legal emancipation of users violates Article V.
>
> . . . Parents—and only parents—have the right and the responsibility to restrict the access of their children—and only their children—to library resources. Parents or legal guardians who do not want their children to have access to certain library services, materials or facilities, should so advise their children. Librarians and governing bodies cannot assume the role of parents or the functions of parental authority in the private relationship between parent and child. Librarians and governing bodies have a public and professional obligation to provide equal access to all library resources for all library users.

Policies which set minimum age limits for access to videotapes and/or other audiovisual materials and equipment, with or without parental permission, abridge library use for minors. Further, age limits based on the cost of the materials are unacceptable. Unless directly and specifically prohibited by law from circulating certain motion pictures and video productions to minors, librarians should apply the same standards to circulation of these materials as are applied to books and other materials.

Recognizing that libraries cannot act *in loco parentis*, ALA acknowledges and supports the exercise by parents of their responsibility to guide their own children's reading and viewing. Published reviews of films and videotapes and/or reference works which provide information about the content, subject matter, and recommended audiences can be made available in conjunction with nonprint collections to assist parents in guiding their children without implicating the library in censorship. This material may include information provided by video producers and distributors, promotional material on videotape packaging, and Motion Picture Association of America (MPAA) ratings *if they are included on the tape or in the packaging by the original publisher* and/or if they appear in review sources or reference works included in the library's collection. Marking out or removing ratings information from videotape packages constitutes expurgation or censorship.

MPAA and other rating services are private advisory codes and have no legal standing*. For the library to add such ratings to the materials if they are not already there, to post a list of such ratings with a collection, or to attempt to enforce such ratings through circulation policies or other procedures constitutes labeling, "an attempt to prejudice attitudes" about the material, and is unacceptable. The application of locally generated ratings schemes intended to provide content warnings to library users is also inconsistent with the LIBRARY BILL OF RIGHTS.

*For information on case law, please contact the ALA Office for Intellectual Freedom.

See also: STATEMENT ON LABELING and EXPURGATION OF LIBRARY MATERIALS, Interpretations of the LIBRARY BILL OF RIGHTS.

Adopted June 28, 1989, by the ALA Council; the quotation from FREE ACCESS TO LIBRARIES FOR MINORS was changed after Council adopted the July 3, 1991, revision of that Interpretation.

Reprinted by permission of the American Library Association

ACCESS TO LIBRARY RESOURCES AND SERVICES REGARDLESS OF GENDER OR SEXUAL ORIENTATION

An Interpretation of the Library Bill of Rights

American libraries exist and function within the context of a body of laws derived from the United States Constitution and the First Amendment. The LIBRARY BILL OF RIGHTS embodies the basic policies which guide libraries in the provision of services, materials and programs.

In the preamble to its LIBRARY BILL OF RIGHTS, the American Library Association affirms that *all* [emphasis added] libraries are forums for information and ideas. This concept of *forum* and its accompanying principle of *inclusiveness* pervade all six articles of the LIBRARY BILL OF RIGHTS.

The American Library Association stringently and unequivocally maintains that libraries and librarians have an obligation to resist efforts that systematically exclude materials dealing with any subject matter, including gender, homosexuality, bisexuality, lesbianism, heterosexuality, gay lifestyles, or any facet of sexual orientation:

- Article I of the LIBRARY BILL OF RIGHTS states that "Materials should not be excluded because of the origin, background, or views of those contributing to their creation." The Association affirms that books and other materials coming from gay presses, gay, lesbian, or bisexual authors or other creators, and materials dealing with gay lifestyles are protected by the LIBRARY BILL OF RIGHTS. Librarians are obligated by the LIBRARY BILL OF RIGHTS to endeavor to select materials without regard to the gender or sexual orientation of their creators by using the criteria identified in their written, approved selection policies (ALA policy 53.1.5).
- Article II maintains that "Libraries should provide materials and information presenting all points of view on current and historical issues. Materials should not be proscribed or removed because of partisan or doctrinal disapproval." Library services, materials, and programs representing diverse points of view on gender or sexual orientation should be considered for purchase and inclusion in library collections and programs (ALA policies 53.1.1, 53.1.9, and 53.1.11). The Association affirms that attempts to proscribe or remove materials dealing with gay or lesbian life without regard to the written, approved

selection policy violate this tenet and constitute censorship.

- Articles III and IV mandate that libraries "challenge censorship" and cooperate with those "resisting abridgement of free expression and free access to ideas."
- Article V holds that "A person's right to use a library should not be denied or abridged because of origin, age, background or views." In the LIBRARY BILL OF RIGHTS and all its interpretations, it is intended that: "origin" encompasses all the characteristics of individuals that are inherent in the circumstances of their birth; "age" encompasses all the characteristics of individuals that are inherent in their levels of development and maturity; "background" encompasses all the characteristics of individuals that are a result of their life experiences; and "views" encompasses all the opinions and beliefs held and expressed by individuals.
Therefore, Article V of the LIBRARY BILL OF RIGHTS mandates that library services, materials, and programs be available to all members of the community the library serves, without regard to gender or sexual orientation.
- Article VI maintains that "Libraries which make exhibit spaces and meeting rooms available to the public they serve should make such facilities available on an equitable basis, regardless of the beliefs or affiliations of individuals or groups requesting their use." This protection extends to all groups and members of the community the library serves, without regard to gender or sexual orientation.

The American Library Association holds that any attempt, be it legal or extra-legal, to regulate or suppress library services, materials, or programs must be resisted in order that protected expression is not abridged. Librarians have a professional obligation to ensure that all library users have free and equal access to the entire range of library services, materials, and programs. Therefore, the Association strongly opposes any effort to limit access to information and ideas. The Association also encourages librarians to proactively support the First Amendment rights of all library users, including gays, lesbians, and bisexuals.

Adopted by the ALA Council, June 30, 1993.

Reprinted by permission of the American Library Association

ACCESS TO RESOURCES AND SERVICES IN THE SCHOOL LIBRARY MEDIA PROGRAM

An Interpretation of the Library Bill of Rights

The school library media program plays a unique role in promoting intellectual freedom. It serves as a point of voluntary access to information and ideas and as a learning laboratory for students as they acquire critical thinking and problem solving skills needed in a pluralistic society. Although the educational level and program of the school necessarily shapes the resources and services of a school library media program, the principles of the LIBRARY BILL OF RIGHTS apply equally to all libraries, including school library media programs.

School library media professionals assume a leadership role in promoting the principles of intellectual freedom within the school by providing resources and services that create and sustain an atmosphere of free inquiry. School library media professionals work closely with teachers to integrate instructional activities in classroom units designed to equip students to locate, evaluate, and use a broad range of ideas effectively. Through resources, programming, and educational processes, students and teachers experience the free and robust debate characteristic of a democratic society.

School library media professionals cooperate with other individuals in building collections of resources appropriate to the developmental and maturity levels of students. These collections provide resources which support the curriculum and are consistent with the philosophy, goals, and objectives of the school district. Resources in school library media collections represent diverse points of view and current as well as historical issues.

While English is, by history and tradition, the customary language of the United States, the languages in use in any given community may vary. Schools serving communities in which other languages are used make efforts to accommodate the needs of students for whom English is a second language. To support these efforts, and to ensure equal access to resources and services, the school library media program provides resources which reflect the linguistic pluralism of the community.

Members of the school community involved in the collection development process employ educational criteria to select resources unfettered by their personal, political, social, or religious views. Students and educators served by the school library media program have access to resources and services free of constraints resulting from personal, partisan, or doctrinal disapproval. School library media professionals resist efforts by individuals to define what is appropriate for all students or teachers to read, view, or hear.

Major barriers between students and resources include: imposing age or grade level restrictions on the use of resources, limiting the use of interlibrary loan and access to electronic information, charging fees for information in specific formats, requiring permissions from parents or teachers, establishing restricted shelves or closed collections, and labeling. Policies, procedures, and rules related to the use of resources and services support free and open access to information.

The school board adopts policies that guarantee students access to a broad range of ideas. These include policies on collection development and procedures for the review of resources about which concerns have been raised. Such policies, developed by persons in the school community, provide for a timely and fair hearing and assure that procedures are applied equitably to all expressions of concern.

School library media professionals implement district policies and procedures in the school.

Adopted July 2, 1986; amended January 10, 1990, by the ALA Council.

Reprinted by permission of the American Library Association

CHALLENGED MATERIALS

An Interpretation of the Library Bill of Rights

The American Library Association declares as a matter of firm principle that it is the responsibility of every library to have a clearly defined materials selection policy in written form which reflects the LIBRARY BILL OF RIGHTS, and which is approved by the appropriate governing authority.

Challenged materials which meet the criteria for selection in the materials selection policy of the library should not be removed under any legal or extra-legal pressure. The LIBRARY BILL OF RIGHTS states in Article I that "Materials should not be excluded because of the origin, background, or views of those contributing to their creation," and in Article II, that "Materials should not be proscribed or removed because of partisan or doctrinal disapproval." Freedom of expression is protected by the Constitution of the United States, but constitutionally protected expression is often separated from unprotected expression only by a dim and uncertain line. The Constitution requires a procedure designed to focus searchingly on challenged expression before it can be suppressed. An adversary hearing is a part of this procedure.

Therefore, any attempt, be it legal or extra-legal, to regulate or suppress materials in libraries must be closely scrutinized to the end that protected expression is not abridged.

Adopted June 25, 1971; amended July 1, 1981; amended January 10, 1990, by the ALA Council.

Reprinted by permission of the American Library Association

DIVERSITY IN COLLECTION DEVELOPMENT

An Interpretation of the Library Bill of Rights

Throughout history, the focus of censorship has fluctuated from generation to generation. Books and other materials have not been selected or have been removed from library collections for many reasons, among which are prejudicial language and ideas, political content, economic theory, social philosophies, religious beliefs, sexual forms of expression, and other topics of a potentially controversial nature.

Some examples of censorship may include removing or not selecting materials because they are considered by some as racist or sexist; not purchasing conservative religious materials; not selecting materials about or by minorities because it is thought these groups or interests are not represented in a community; or not providing information on or materials from non-mainstream political entities.

Librarians may seek to increase user awareness of materials on various social concerns by many means, including, but not limited to, issuing bibliographies and presenting exhibits and programs.

Librarians have a professional responsibility to be inclusive, not exclusive, in collection development and in the provision of interlibrary loan. Access to all materials legally obtainable should be assured to the user, and policies should not unjustly exclude materials even if they are offensive to the librarian or the user. Collection development should reflect the philosophy inherent in Article II of the LIBRARY BILL OF RIGHTS: "Libraries should provide materials and information presenting all points of view on current and historical issues. Materials should not be proscribed or removed because of partisan or doctrinal disapproval." A balanced collection reflects a diversity of materials, not an equality of numbers. Collection development responsibilities include selecting materials in the languages in common use in the community which the library serves. Collection development and the selection of materials should be done according to professional standards and established selection and review procedures.

There are many complex facets to any issue, and variations of context in which issues may be expressed, discussed, or interpreted. Librarians have a professional responsibility to be fair, just, and equitable and to give all library users equal protection in guarding against violation of the library patron's right to read, view, or listen to materials and resources protected by the First Amendment, no matter what the viewpoint of the author, creator, or selector. Librarians have an obligation to protect library collections from removal of materials based on personal bias or prejudice, and to select and support the access to materials on all subjects that meet, as closely as possible, the needs and interests of all persons in the community which the library serves. This includes materials that reflect political, economic, religious, social, minority, and sexual issues.

Intellectual freedom, the essence of equitable library services, provides for free access to all expressions of ideas through which any and all sides of a question, cause, or movement may be explored. Toleration is meaningless without tolerance for what some may consider detestable. Librarians cannot justly permit their own preferences to limit their degree of tolerance in collection development, because freedom is indivisible.

Adopted July 14, 1982; amended January 10, 1990, by the ALA Council.

Reprinted by permission of the American Library Association

ECONOMIC BARRIERS TO INFORMATION ACCESS

An Interpretation of the Library Bill of Rights

A democracy presupposes an informed citizenry. The First Amendment mandates the right of all persons to free expression, and the corollary right to receive the constitutionally protected expression of others. The publicly supported library provides free and equal access to information for all people of the community the library serves. While the roles, goals and objectives of publicly supported libraries may differ, they share this common mission.

The library's essential mission must remain the first consideration for librarians and governing bodies faced with economic pressures and competition for funding.

In support of this mission, the American Library Association has enumerated certain principles of library services in the LIBRARY BILL OF RIGHTS.

Principles Governing Fines, Fees and User Charges

Article I of the LIBRARY BILL OF RIGHTS states: "Books and other library resources should be provided for the interest, information, and enlightenment of all people of the community the library serves."

Article V of the LIBRARY BILL OF RIGHTS states: "A person's right to use a library should not be denied or abridged because of origin, age, background, or views."

The American Library Association opposes the charging of user fees for the provision of information by all libraries and information services that receive their major support from public funds. All information resources that are provided directly or indirectly by the library, regardless of technology, format, or methods of delivery, should be readily, equally and equitably accessible to all library users.

Libraries that adhere to these principles systematically monitor their programs of service for potential barriers to access and strive to eliminate such barriers when they occur. All library policies and procedures, particularly those involving fines, fees, or other user charges, should be scrutinized for potential barriers to access. All services should be designed and implemented with care, so as not to infringe on or interfere with the provision or delivery of information and resources for all users. Services should be re-evaluated on a regular basis to ensure that the library's basic mission remains uncompromised.

Librarians and governing bodies should look for alternative

models and methods of library administration that minimize distinctions among users based on their economic status or financial condition. They should resist the temptation to impose user fees to alleviate financial pressures, at long term cost to institutional integrity and public confidence in libraries.

Library services that involve the provision of information, regardless of format, technology, or method of delivery, should be made available to all library users on an equal and equitable basis. Charging fees for the use of library collections, services, programs, or facilities that were purchased with public funds raises barriers to access. Such fees effectively abridge or deny access for some members of the community because they reinforce distinctions among users based on their ability and willingness to pay.

Principles Governing Conditions of Funding

Article II of the LIBRARY BILL OF RIGHTS states: "Materials should not be proscribed or removed because of partisan or doctrinal disapproval."

Article III of the LIBRARY BILL OF RIGHTS states: "Libraries should challenge censorship in the fulfillment of their responsibility to provide information and enlightenment."

Article IV of the LIBRARY BILL OF RIGHTS states: "Libraries should cooperate with all persons and groups concerned with resisting abridgment of free expression and free access to ideas."

The American Library Association opposes any legislative or regulatory attempt to impose content restrictions on library resources, or to limit user access to information, as a condition of funding for publicly supported libraries and information services.

The First Amendment guarantee of freedom of expression is violated when the right to receive that expression is subject to arbitrary restrictions based on content.

Librarians and governing bodies should examine carefully any terms or conditions attached to library funding and should oppose attempts to limit through such conditions full and equal access to information because of content. This principle applies equally to private gifts or bequests and to public funds. In particular, librarians and governing bodies have an obligation to reject such restrictions when the effect of the restriction is to limit equal and equitable access to information.

Librarians and governing bodies should cooperate with all efforts to create a community consensus that publicly supported libraries require funding unfettered by restrictions. Such a consensus supports the library mission to provide the free and unrestricted exchange of information and ideas necessary to a functioning democracy.

The Association's historic position in this regard is stated clearly in a number of Association policies: 50.4 *Free Access to Information*, 50.9 *Financing of Libraries*, 51.2 *Equal Access to Library Service*, 51.3 *Intellectual Freedom*, 53 *Intellectual Freedom Policies*, 59.1 *Policy Objectives*, and 60 *Library Services for the Poor.*

Adopted by the ALA Council, June 30, 1993.

Reprinted by permission of the American Library Association

EVALUATING LIBRARY COLLECTIONS

An Interpretation of the Library Bill of Rights

The continuous review of library materials is necessary as a means of maintaining an active library collection of current interest to users. In the process, materials may be added and physically deteriorated or obsolete materials may be replaced or removed in accordance with the collection maintenance policy of a given library and the needs of the community it serves. Continued evaluation is closely related to the goals and responsibilities of libraries and is a valuable tool of collection development. This procedure is not to be used as a convenient means to remove materials presumed to be controversial or disapproved of by segments of the community. Such abuse of the evaluation function violates the principles of intellectual freedom and is in opposition to the Preamble and Articles 1 and 2 of the LIBRARY BILL OF RIGHTS, which state:

> The American Library Association affirms that all libraries are forums for information and ideas, and that the following basic policies should guide their services.
>
> 1. Books and other library resources should be provided for the interest, information, and enlightenment of all people of the community the library serves. Materials should not be excluded because of the origin, background, or views of those contributing to their creation.
> 2. Libraries should provide materials and information presenting all points of view on current and historical issues. Materials should not be proscribed or removed because of partisan or doctrinal disapproval.

The American Library Association opposes such "silent censorship" and strongly urges that libraries adopt guidelines setting forth the positive purposes and principles of evaluation of materials in library collections.

Adopted February 2, 1973; amended July 1, 1981, by the ALA Council.

Reprinted by permission of the American Library Association

EXHIBIT SPACES AND BULLETIN BOARDS

An Interpretation of the Library Bill of Rights

Libraries often provide exhibit spaces and bulletin boards. The uses made of these spaces should conform to the LIBRARY BILL OF RIGHTS: Article I states, "Materials should not be excluded because of the origin, background, or views of those contributing to their creation." Article II states, "Materials should not be proscribed or removed because of partisan or doctrinal disapproval." Article VI maintains that exhibit space should be made available "on an equitable basis, regardless of the beliefs or affiliations of individuals or groups requesting their use."

In developing library exhibits, staff members should endeavor to present a broad spectrum of opinion and a variety of viewpoints. Libraries should not shrink from developing exhibits because of controversial content or because of the beliefs or affiliations of those whose work is represented. Just as libraries do not endorse the viewpoints of those whose works are represented in their collections, libraries also do not endorse the beliefs or viewpoints of topics which may be the subject of library exhibits.

Exhibit areas often are made available for use by community groups. Libraries should formulate a written policy for the use of these exhibit areas to assure that space is provided on an equitable basis to all groups which request it.

Written policies for exhibit space use should be stated in inclusive rather than exclusive terms. For example, a policy that the library's exhibit space is open "to organizations engaged in educational, cultural, intellectual, or charitable activities" is an inclusive statement of the limited uses of the exhibit space. This defined limitation would permit religious groups to use the exhibit space because they engage in intellectual activities, but would exclude most commercial uses of the exhibit space.

A publicly supported library may limit use of its exhibit space to strictly "library-related" activities, provided that the limitation is clearly circumscribed and is viewpoint neutral.

Libraries may include in this policy rules regarding the time, place, and manner of use of the exhibit space, so long as the rules are content-neutral and are applied in the same manner to all groups wishing to use the space. A library may wish to limit access to exhibit space to groups within the community served by the library. This practice is acceptable provided that the same rules and regulations apply to everyone, and that exclusion is not made on the basis of the doctrinal, religious, or political beliefs of the potential users.

The library should not censor or remove an exhibit because some members of the community may disagree with its content. Those who object to the content of any exhibit held at the library should be able to submit their complaint and/or their own exhibit proposal to be judged according to the policies established by the library.

Libraries may wish to post a permanent notice near the exhibit area stating that the library does not advocate or endorse the viewpoints of exhibits or exhibitors.

Libraries which make bulletin boards available to public groups for posting notices of public interest should develop criteria for the use of these spaces based on the same considerations as those outlined above. Libraries may wish to develop criteria regarding the size of material to be displayed, the length of time materials may remain on the bulletin board, the frequency with which material may be posted for the same group, and the geographic area from which notices will be accepted.

Adopted July 2, 1991, by the ALA Council.

Reprinted by permission of the American Library Association

EXPURGATION OF LIBRARY MATERIALS

An Interpretation of the Library Bill of Rights

Expurgating library materials is a violation of the LIBRARY BILL OF RIGHTS. Expurgation as defined by this interpretation includes any deletion, excision, alteration, editing, or obliteration of any part(s) of books or other library resources by the library, its agent, or its parent institution (if any). By such expurgation, the library is in effect denying access to the complete work and the entire spectrum of ideas that the work intended to express. Such action stands in violation of Articles 1, 2, and 3 of the LIBRARY BILL OF RIGHTS, which state that "Materials should not be excluded because of the origin, background, or views of those contributing to their creation," that "Materials should not be proscribed or removed because of partisan or doctrinal disapproval," and that "Libraries should challenge censorship in the fulfillment of their responsibility to provide information and enlightenment."

The act of expurgation has serious implications. It involves a determination that it is necessary to restrict access to the complete work. This is censorship. When a work is expurgated, under the assumption that certain portions of that work would be harmful to minors, the situation is no less serious.

Expurgation of any books or other library resources imposes a restriction, without regard to the rights and desires of all library users, by limiting access to ideas and information.

Further, expurgation without written permission from the holder of the copyright on the material may violate the copyright provisions of the United States Code.

Adopted February 2, 1973; amended July 1, 1981; amended January 10, 1990, by the ALA Council.

Reprinted by permission of the American Library Association

FREE ACCESS TO LIBRARIES FOR MINORS

An Interpretation of the Library Bill of Rights

Library policies and procedures which effectively deny minors equal access to all library resources available to other users violate the LIBRARY BILL OF RIGHTS. The American Library Association opposes all attempts to restrict access to library services, materials, and facilities based on the age of library users.

Article V of the LIBRARY BILL OF RIGHTS states, "A person's right to use a library should not be denied or abridged because of origin, age, background, or views." The "right to use a library" includes free access to, and unrestricted use of, all the services, materials, and facilities the library has to offer. Every restriction on access to, and use of, library resources, based solely on the chronological age, educational level, or legal emancipation of users violates Article V.

Libraries are charged with the mission of developing resources to meet the diverse information needs and interests of the communities they serve. Services, materials, and facilities which fulfill the needs and interests of library users at different stages in their personal development are a necessary part of library resources. The needs and interests of each library user, and resources appropriate to meet those needs and interests, must be determined on an individual basis. Librarians cannot predict what resources will best fulfill the needs and interests of any individual user based on a single criterion such as chronological age, level of education, or legal emancipation.

The selection and development of library resources should not be diluted because of minors having the same access to library resources as adult users. Institutional self-censorship diminishes the credibility of the library in the community, and restricts access for all library users.

Librarians and governing bodies should not resort to age restrictions on access to library resources in an effort to avoid actual or anticipated objections from parents or anyone else. The mission, goals, and objectives of libraries do not authorize librarians or governing bodies to assume, abrogate, or overrule the rights and responsibilities of parents or legal guardians. Librarians and governing bodies should maintain that parents—and only parents—have the right and the responsibility to restrict the access of their children—and only their children—to library resources. Parents or legal guardians who do not want their children to have access to certain library services, materials or facilities, should so advise their children. Librarians and governing bodies cannot assume the role of parents or the functions of parental authority in the private relationship between parent and child. Librarians and governing bodies have a public and professional obligation to provide equal access to all library resources for all library users.

Librarians have a professional commitment to ensure that all members of the community they serve have free and equal access to the entire range of library resources regardless of content, approach, format, or amount of detail. This principle of library service applies equally to all users, minors as well as adults. Librarians and governing bodies must uphold this principle in order to provide adequate and effective service to minors.

Adopted June 30, 1972; amended July 1, 1981; July 3, 1991, by the ALA Council.

Reprinted by permission of the American Library Association

LIBRARY INITIATED PROGRAMS AS A RESOURCE

An Interpretation of the Library Bill of Rights

Library initiated programs support the mission of the library by providing users with additional opportunities for information, education and recreation. Article 1 of the LIBRARY BILL OF RIGHTS states: "Books and other library resources should be provided for the interest, information and enlightenment of all people of the community the library serves."

Library initiated programs take advantage of library staff expertise, collections, services and facilities to increase access to information and information resources. Library initiated programs introduce users and potential users to the resources of the library and to the library's primary function as a facilitator of information access. The library may participate in cooperative or joint programs with other agencies, organizations, institutions or individuals as part of its own effort to address information needs and to facilitate information access in the community the library serves.

Library initiated programs on site and in other locations include, but are not limited to, speeches, community forums, discussion groups, demonstrations, displays, and live or media presentations.

Libraries serving multilingual or multicultural communities make efforts to accommodate the information needs of those for whom English is a second language. Library initiated programs across language and cultural barriers introduce otherwise unserved populations to the resources of the library and provide access to information.

Library initiated programs "should not be proscribed or removed (or canceled) because of partisan or doctrinal disapproval" of the contents of the program or the views expressed by the participants, as stated in Article 2 of the LIBRARY BILL OF RIGHTS. Library sponsorship of a program does not constitute an endorsement of the content of the program or the views expressed by the participants, any more than the purchase of material for the library collection constitutes an endorsement of the contents of the material or the views of its creator.

Library initiated programs are a library resource, and as such, are developed in accordance with written guidelines, as approved and adopted by the library's policy-making body. These guidelines include an endorsement of the LIBRARY BILL OF RIGHTS and set forth the library's commitment to free and open access to information and ideas for all users.

Library staff select topics, speakers and resource materials for library initiated programs based on the interests and information needs of the community. Topics, speakers and resource materials are not excluded from library initiated programs because of possible controversy. Concerns, questions or complaints about library initiated program are handled according to the same written policy and procedures which govern reconsiderations of other library resources.

Library initiated programs are offered free of charge and are open to all. Article 5 of the LIBRARY BILL OF RIGHTS states: "A person's right to use a library should not be denied or abridged because of origin, age, background, or views."

The "right to use a library" encompasses all of the resources the library offers, including the right to attend library initiated programs. Libraries do not deny or abridge access to library resources, including library initiated programs, based on an individual's economic background and ability to pay.

Adopted January 27, 1982. Amended June 26, 1990, by the ALA Council.

Reprinted by permission of the American Library Association

MEETING ROOMS

An Interpretation of the Library Bill of Rights

Many libraries provide meeting rooms for individuals and groups as part of a program of service. Article VI of the LIBRARY BILL OF RIGHTS states that such facilities should be made available to the public served by the given library "on an equitable basis, regardless of the beliefs or affiliations of individuals or groups requesting their use."

Libraries maintaining meeting room facilities should develop and publish policy statements governing use. These statements can properly define time, place, or manner of use; such qualifications should not pertain to the content of a meeting or to the beliefs or affiliations of the sponsors. These statements should be made available in any commonly used language within the community served.

If meeting rooms in libraries supported by public funds are made available to the general public for non-library sponsored events, the library may not exclude any group based on the subject matter to be discussed or based on the ideas that the group advocates. For example, if a library allows charities and sports clubs to discuss their activities in library meeting rooms, then the library should not exclude partisan political or religious groups from discussing their activities in the same facilities. If a library opens its meeting rooms to a wide variety of civic organizations, then the library may not deny access to a religious organization. Libraries may wish to post a permanent notice near the meeting room stating that the library does not advocate or endorse the viewpoints of meetings or meeting room users.

Written policies for meeting room use should be stated in inclusive rather than exclusive terms. For example, a policy that the library's facilities are open "to organizations engaged in educational, cultural, intellectual, or charitable activities" is an inclusive statement of the limited uses to which the facilities may be put. This defined limitation would permit religious groups to use the facilities because they engage in intellectual activities, but would exclude most commercial uses of the facility.

A publicly supported library may limit use of its meeting rooms to strictly "library-related" activities, provided that the limitation is clearly circumscribed and is viewpoint neutral.

Written policies may include limitations on frequency of use, and whether or not meetings held in library meeting rooms must be open to the public. If state and local laws permit private as well as public sessions of meetings in libraries, libraries may choose to offer both options. The same standard should be applicable to all.

If meetings are open to the public, libraries should include in their meeting room policy statement a section which addresses admission fees. If admission fees are permitted, libraries shall seek to make it possible that these fees do not limit access to individuals who may be unable to pay, but who wish to attend the meeting. Article V of the LIBRARY BILL OF RIGHTS states that "a person's right to use a library should not be denied or abridged because of origin, age, background, or views." It is inconsistent with Article V to restrict indirectly access to library meeting rooms based on an individual's or group's ability to pay for that access.

Adopted July 2, 1991, by the ALA Council.

Reprinted by permission of the American Library Association

RESTRICTED ACCESS TO LIBRARY MATERIALS

An Interpretation of the Library Bill of Rights

Libraries are a traditional forum for the open exchange of information. Attempts to restrict access to library materials violate the basic tenets of the LIBRARY BILL OF RIGHTS.

Historically, attempts have been made to limit access by relegating materials into segregated collections. These attempts are in violation of established policy. Such collections are often referred to by a variety of names, including "closed shelf," "locked case," "adults only," "restricted shelf," or "high demand." Access to some materials also may require a monetary fee or financial deposit. In any situation which restricts access to certain materials, a barrier is placed between the patron and those materials. That barrier may be age related, linguistic, economic, or psychological in nature.

Because materials placed in restricted collections often deal with controversial, unusual, or "sensitive" subjects, having to ask a librarian or circulation clerk for them may be embarrassing or inhibiting for patrons desiring the materials. Needing to ask for materials may pose a language barrier or a staff service barrier. Because restricted collections often are composed of materials which some library patrons consider "objectionable," the potential user may be predisposed to think of the materials as "objectionable" and, therefore, are reluctant to ask for them.

Barriers between the materials and the patron which are psychological, or are affected by language skills, are nonetheless limitations on access to information. Even when a title is listed in the catalog with a reference to its restricted status, a barrier is placed between the patron and the publication (see also "Statement on Labeling").

There may be, however, countervailing factors to establish policies to protect library materials—specifically, for reasons of physical preservation including protection from theft or mutilation. Any such policies must be carefully formulated and administered with extreme attention to the principles of intellectual freedom. This caution is also in keeping with ALA policies, such as "Evaluating Library Collections," "Free Access to Libraries for Minors," and the "Preservation Policy."

Finally, in keeping with the "Joint Statement on Access" of the American Library Association and Society of American Archivists, restrictions that result from donor agreements or contracts for special collections materials must be similarly circumscribed. Permanent exclusions are not acceptable. The overriding impetus must be to work for free and unfettered access to all documentary heritage.

Adopted February 2, 1973; amended July 1, 1981; July 3, 1991, by the ALA Council.

Reprinted by permission of the American Library Association

<h1 align="center">STATEMENT ON LABELING</h1>

<h2 align="center">An Interpretation of the Library Bill of Rights</h2>

Labeling is the practice of describing or designating materials by affixing a prejudicial label and/or segregating them by a prejudicial system. The American Library Association opposes these means of predisposing people's attitudes toward library materials for the following reasons:

1. Labeling is an attempt to prejudice attitudes and as such, it is a censor's tool.
2. Some find it easy and even proper, according to their ethics, to establish criteria for judging publications as objectionable. However, injustice and ignorance rather than justice and enlightenment result from such practices, and the American Library Association opposes the establishment of such criteria.
3. Libraries do not advocate the ideas found in their collections. The presence of books and other resources in a library does not indicate endorsement of their contents by the library.

A variety of private organizations promulgate rating systems and/or review materials as a means of advising either their members or the general public concerning their opinions of the contents and suitability or appropriate age for use of certain books, films, recordings, or other materials. For the library to adopt or enforce any of these private systems, to attach such ratings to library materials, to include them in bibliographic records, library catalogs, or other finding aids, or otherwise to endorse them would violate the LIBRARY BILL OF RIGHTS.

While some attempts have been made to adopt these systems into law, the constitutionality of such measures is extremely questionable. If such legislation is passed which applies within a library's jurisdiction, the library should seek competent legal advice concerning its applicability to library operations.

Publishers, industry groups, and distributors sometimes add ratings to material or include them as part of their packaging. Librarians should not endorse such practices. However, removing or obliterating such ratings—if placed there by or with permission of the copyright holder—could constitute expurgation, which is also unacceptable.

The American Library Association opposes efforts which aim at closing any path to knowledge. This statement, however, does not exclude the adoption of organizational schemes designed as directional aids or to facilitate access to materials.

Adopted July 13, 1951. Amended June 25, 1971; July 1, 1981; June 26, 1990, by the ALA Council.

Reprinted by permission of the American Library Association

THE UNIVERSAL RIGHT TO FREE EXPRESSION

An Interpretation of the Library Bill of Rights

Freedom of expression is an inalienable human right and the foundation for self-government. Freedom of expression encompasses the freedoms of speech, press, religion, assembly, and association, and the corollary right to receive information.

The American Library Association endorses this principle, which is also set forth in the UNIVERSAL DECLARATION OF HUMAN RIGHTS, adopted by the United Nations General Assembly. The Preamble of this document states that " ... recognition of the inherent dignity and of the equal and inalienable rights of all members of the human family is the foundation of freedom, justice, and peace in the world ... " and " ... the advent of a world in which human beings shall enjoy freedom of speech and belief and freedom from fear and want has been proclaimed as the highest aspiration of the common people. ... "
Article 18 of this document states:

Everyone has the right to freedom of thought, conscience and religion; this right includes freedom to change his religion or belief, and freedom, either alone or in community with others and in public or private, to manifest his religion or belief in teaching, practice, worship and observance.

Article 19 states:

Everyone has the right to freedom of opinion and expression; this right includes freedom to hold opinions without interference and to seek, receive and impart information and ideas through any media regardless of frontiers.

Article 20 states:

1. Everyone has the right to freedom of peaceful assembly and association.
2. No one may be compelled to belong to an association.

We affirm our belief that these are inalienable rights of every person, regardless of origin, age, background, or views. We embody our professional commitment to these principles in the LI-BRARY BILL OF RIGHTS and CODE OF PROFESSIONAL ETHICS, as adopted by the American Library Association.

We maintain that these are universal principles and should be applied by libraries and librarians throughout the world. The American Library Association's policy on International Relations reflects these objectives: " . . . to encourage the exchange, dissemination, and access to information and the unrestricted flow of library materials in all formats throughout the world."

We know that censorship, ignorance, and limitations on the free flow of information are the tools of tyranny and oppression. We believe that ideas and information topple the walls of hate and fear and build bridges of cooperation and understanding far more effectively than weapons and armies.

The American Library Association is unswerving in its commitment to human rights and intellectual freedom; the two are inseparably linked and inextricably entwined. Freedom of opinion and expression is not derived from or dependent on any form of government or political power. This right is inherent in every individual. It cannot be surrendered, nor can it be denied. True justice comes from the exercise of this right.

We recognize the power of information and ideas to inspire justice, to restore freedom and dignity to the oppressed, and to change the hearts and minds of the oppressors.

Courageous men and women, in difficult and dangerous circumstances throughout human history, have demonstrated that freedom lives in the human heart and cries out for justice even in the face of threats, enslavement, imprisonment, torture, exile, and death. We draw inspiration from their example. They challenge us to remain steadfast in our most basic professional responsibility to promote and defend the right of free expression.

There is no good censorship. Any effort to restrict free expression and the free flow of information aids the oppressor. Fighting oppression with censorship is self-defeating.

Threats to the freedom of expression of any person anywhere are threats to the freedom of all people everywhere. Violations of human rights and the right of free expression have been recorded in virtually every country and society across the globe.

In response to these violations, we affirm these principles:

- The American Library Association opposes any use of governmental prerogative that leads to the intimidation of individuals which prevents them from exercising their rights to hold opinions without interference, and to seek, receive, and impart information and ideas. We urge libraries and librarians everywhere to resist such abuse of governmental power, and to support those against whom such governmental power has been employed.

- The American Library Association condemns any governmental effort to involve libraries and librarians in restrictions on the right of any individual to hold opinions without interference, and to seek, receive, and impart information and ideas. Such restrictions pervert the function of the library and violate the professional responsibilities of librarians.
- The American Library Association rejects censorship in any form. Any action which denies the inalienable human rights of individuals only damages the will to resist oppression, strengthens the hand of the oppressor, and undermines the cause of justice.
- The American Library Association will not abrogate these principles. We believe that censorship corrupts the cause of justice, and contributes to the demise of freedom.

Adopted by the ALA Council, January 16, 1991.

Reprinted by permission of the American Library Association

POLICY CONCERNING CONFIDENTIALITY OF PERSONALLY IDENTIFIABLE INFORMATION ABOUT LIBRARY USERS

The ethical responsibilities of librarians, as well as statutes in most states and the District of Columbia, protect the privacy of library users. Confidentiality extends to "information sought or received, and materials consulted, borrowed or acquired," and includes database search records, reference interviews, circulation records, interlibrary loan records, and other personally identifiable uses of library materials, facilities, or services.

The First Amendment's guarantee of freedom of speech and of the press requires that the corresponding rights to hear what is spoken and read what is written be preserved, free from fear of government intrusion, intimidation, or reprisal. The American Library Association reaffirms its opposition to "any use of government prerogatives which lead to the intimidation of the individual or the citizenry from the exercise of free expression...[and] encourages resistance to such abuse of government power...." (ALA Policy 53.4). In seeking access or in the pursuit of information, confidentiality is the primary means of providing the privacy that will free the individual from fear of intimidation or retaliation.

Libraries are one of the great bulwarks of democracy. They are living embodiments of the First Amendment because their collections include voices of dissent as well as assent. Libraries are impartial resources providing information on all points of view, available to all persons regardless of age, race, religion, national origin, social or political views, economic status, or any other characteristic. The role of libraries as such a resource must not be compromised by an erosion of the privacy rights of library users.

The American Library Association regularly receives reports of visits by agents of federal, state, and local law enforcement agencies to libraries, where it is alleged they have asked for personally identifiable information about library users. These visits, whether under the rubric of simply informing libraries of agency concerns or for some other reason, reflect an insensitivity to the legal and ethical bases for confidentiality, and the role it plays in the preservation of First Amendment rights, rights also extended to foreign nationals while in the United States. The government's interest in library use reflects a dangerous and fallacious equation of what a person reads with what that person believes or how that person is likely to behave. Such a presumption can and does threaten the freedom of access to information. It also is a threat to a crucial aspect of First Amendment rights: that freedom of speech and of the press include the freedom to hold, disseminate and receive unpopular, minority, "extreme," or even "dangerous" ideas.

The American Library Association recognizes that, under limited circumstances, access to certain information might be restricted due to a legitimate "national security" concern. However, there has been no showing of a plausible probability that national security will be compromised by any use made of *unclassified* information available in libraries. Thus, the right of access to this information by individuals, including foreign nationals, must be recognized as part of the librarian's legal and ethical responsibility to protect the confidentiality of the library user.

The American Library Association also recognizes that law enforcement agencies and officers may occasionally believe that library records contain information which would be helpful to the investigation of criminal activity. If there is a reasonable basis to believe such records are *necessary* to the progress of an investigation or prosecution, the American judicial system provides the mechanism for seeking release of such confidential records: the issuance of a court order, following a showing of *good cause* based on *specific facts*, by a court of competent jurisdiction.

Adopted July 2, 1991, by the ALA Council.

Reprinted by permission of the American Library Association

GUIDELINES FOR THE DEVELOPMENT AND IMPLEMENTATION OF POLICIES, REGULATIONS AND PROCEDURES AFFECTING ACCESS TO LIBRARY MATERIALS, SERVICES AND FACILITIES

Introduction

Publicly supported libraries exist within the context of a body of law derived from the United States Constitution and appropriate state constitutions, defined by statute, and implemented by regulations, policies and procedures established by their governing bodies and administrations. These regulations, policies and procedures establish the mission of the library, define its functions, services and operations and ascertain the rights and responsibilities of the clientele served by the library.

Publicly supported library service is based upon the First Amendment right of free expression. The publicly supported library provides free and equal access to information for all people of the community it serves. Thus, publicly supported libraries are governmental agencies designated as limited public forums for access to information. Libraries that make meeting rooms, exhibit spaces and/or bulletin boards available for public use are also designated as limited public forums for the exchange of information.

Many libraries adopt administrative policies and procedures regulating the organization and use of library materials, services and facilities. These policies and procedures affect access and may have the effect of restricting, denying or creating barriers to access to the library as a public forum, including the library's resources, facilities and services. Library policies and procedures that impinge upon First Amendment rights are subject to a higher standard of review than may be required in the policies of other public services and facilities.

Policies, procedures or regulations that may result in denying, restricting or creating physical or economic barriers to access to the library's public forum must be based on a compelling government interest. However, library governing authorities may place reasonable and narrowly drawn restrictions on the time, place or manner of access to library resources, services or facilities, provided that such restrictions are not based upon arbitrary distinctions between individuals or classes of individuals.

The American Library Association has adopted the LIBRARY BILL OF RIGHTS and Interpretations of the LIBRARY BILL OF RIGHTS to provide library governing authorities, librarians and other library staff and library users with guidelines on how constitutional principles apply to libraries in the United States of America.

The American Library Association's Intellectual Freedom Committee recommends that publicly supported libraries use the following guidelines, based on constitutional principles, to develop policies, regulations and procedures.

Guidelines

All library policies, regulations and procedures should be carefully examined to determine if they may result in denying, restricting or creating barriers to access. If they may result in such restrictions, they:

1. should be developed and implemented within the legal framework that applies to the library. This includes: the United States Constitution, including the First and Fourteenth Amendments, due process and equal treatment under the law; the applicable state constitution; federal and state civil rights legislation; all other applicable federal, state and local legislation; and applicable case law;
2. should cite statutes or ordinances upon which the authority to make that policy is based, when appropriate;
3. should be developed and implemented within the framework of the Library Bill of Rights and its Interpretations;
4. should be based upon the library's mission and objectives;
5. should only impose restrictions on the access to, or use of library resources, services or facilities when those restrictions are necessary to achieve the library's mission and objectives;
6. should narrowly tailor prohibitions or restrictions, in the rare instances when they are required, so they are not more restrictive than needed to serve their objectives;
7. should attempt to balance competing interests and avoid favoring the majority at the expense of individual rights, or allowing individual users' rights to interfere materially with the majority's rights to free and equal access to library resources, services and facilities;
8. should avoid arbitrary distinctions between individuals or classes of users, and should not have the effect of denying or abridging a person's right to use library resources, services or facilities based upon arbitrary distinctions such as origin, age, background or views;

In the LIBRARY BILL OF RIGHTS and all of its Interpretations, it is intended that: "origin" encompasses all the characteristics of individuals that are inherent in the circumstances of their birth; "age" encompasses all the characteristics of individuals that are inherent in their levels of development and maturity; "background" encompasses all the characteristics of individuals that are a result of their life experiences; and "views" encompasses all the opinions and beliefs held and expressed by individuals;

9. should not target specific users or groups of users based upon an assumption or expectation that such users might engage in behavior that will materially interfere with the achievement of substantial library objectives;
10. must be clearly stated so that a reasonably intelligent person will have fair warning of what is expected;
11. must provide a means of appeal;
12. must be reviewed regularly by the library's governing authority and by its legal counsel;
13. must be communicated clearly and made available in an effective manner to all library users;
14. must be enforced evenhandedly, and not in a manner intended to benefit or disfavor any person or group in an arbitrary or capricious manner;

Libraries should develop an ongoing staff training program designed to foster the understanding of the legal framework and principles underlying library policies and to assist staff in gaining the skill and ability to respond to potentially difficult circumstances in a timely, direct and open manner. This program should include training to develop empathy and understanding of the social and economic problems of some library users;

15. should, if reasonably possible, provide adequate alternative means of access to information for those whose behavior results in the denial or restriction of access to any library resource, service or facility.

Adopted June 28, 1994, by the ALA Intellectual Freedom Committee.

Glossary

Below are definitions of some of the terms used in the Guidelines to assist in understanding the applicable standards:

arbitrary distinctions: inappropriate categorizations of persons, classes of persons, conduct, or things based upon criteria irrelevant to the purpose for which the distinctions are made. For example, a rule intended to regulate the length of time an item may be borrowed should not be based on an irrelevant consideration (arbitrary distinction) such as a personal characteristic of the borrower (height or age).

compelling government interest: a term often used by courts when assessing the burden of government regulation or action upon a fundamental right such as freedom of speech. For such a rule to withstand constitutional challenge, the government must show more than a merely important reason—the reason for the rule must be *compelling*—so important that it outweighs even the most valued and basic freedom it negatively impacts.

limited public forum: a public place designated by the government, or established through tradition, as a place dedicated to a particular type of expression. As in a public forum, only reasonable time, place and manner restrictions on speech within the scope of the designated purpose of the forum, may be imposed. The government may exclude entire categories of speech which do not fall within the designated purpose of the forum, but may not discriminate against particular viewpoints on subjects appropriate to the forum.

materially interfere: a term used by courts to describe the necessary level of intrusion, inconvenience or disruption of an accepted or protected activity caused by certain conduct in order to justify regulation of that conduct. A material interference is much more than mere annoyance—it must be an *actual obstacle* to the exercise of a right.

substantial objectives: goals related to the fundamental mission of a government institution, and not merely incidental to the performance of that mission. Providing free and unrestricted access to a broad selection of materials representing various points of view is a substantial objective of a public library. Having spotless white carpeting is not.

Reprinted by permission of the American Library Association

APPENDIX B:

DADDY'S ROOMMATE DOCUMENTS

This appendix contains documents related to the case study reported in chapter 7. The documents are reprinted by permission of the various individuals and organizations identified on each.

CONTENTS OF THIS APPENDIX

JUNEAU SCHOOL DISTRICT SUPERINTENDENT'S DECISION ON *DADDY'S ROOMMATE*

DATE: October 25, 1993

TO: Complainants and Proponents
              Elementary Principals
              Board Members

FROM: Robert S. Van Slyke, Superintendent

SUBJECT: Findings Regarding *Daddy's Roommate*

Introduction: The publication, *Daddy's Roommate*, by Michael Willhoite, was ordered for District elementary school libraries at the end of the 1992–93 school year. In accordance with established procedures in effect for at least twenty years, librarians consulted reviews of the publication, examined a copy, and concluded that it would be appropriate to have it available in elementary libraries.

The five copies of the publication were received during the summer, at which time the book was called to my attention. After reviewing the book, I called one of the District's librarians and asked about the process used in selecting the item. I also requested that librarians re-examine it to insure its appropriateness for addition to collections. My request was honored and librarians re-affirmed their professional judgments as to the book being suitable for shelving in elementary school libraries. While I was quite certain at the time that the book would generate controversy, I believed it to be important to rely on the local building library collection procedures and the professional judgment of staff to whom the task of selecting materials has been delegated.

Complaints: Initial complaints over *Daddy's Roommate* occurred in the latter part of September, 1993. Pursuant to Board Policy 1240, "Controversial Issues," and the implementing regulation, 1240R of the same title, complainants were asked to meet with the appropriate building principal in order to express the complainants' concerns. If the complainants wished to pursue the matter following the conference with the principal, then the complainants would be provided with complaint forms. Completed forms were to be submitted to the superintendent, who would then arrange for the appointment of a committee to consider the complaints at the building level. Committee composition consisted of the principal, two staff members, and two community members.

The first complaint was filed by an Auke Bay parent, followed by complaints at Glacier Valley and Mendenhall River Schools. Following receipt of the complaints, committee members were selected at each of those sites to address the complaints.

Regulation 1240R provides for the committee to consider the complainant's concerns, to examine the material or procedure in question, and to submit a formal written report to the superintendent. Upon receipt of a recommendation, the superintendent is required to make a decision regarding the disposition of the complaint. Complainants not satisfied with the decision of the superintendent may appeal for a hearing before the Board of Education in accordance with established procedures for public participation in Board meetings.

The Glacier Valley Committee met on October 4. Complainants were notified of the meeting and afforded an opportunity to state objections and concerns.

Mendenhall River staff scheduled a meeting with complainants for Tuesday, October 12. While the intent of the procedures is to consider the specific complaints of persons who had previously completed complaint forms, the Mendenhall meeting was attended by a crowd which was estimated to be in excess of 300 persons. A large group attended the meeting of the Auke Bay committee on October 13 as well.

During the week of October 18–22, the first complaint was received by Harborview staff. To date, no complaints have been registered at Gastineau School.

Recommendations: Committee recommendations at Auke Bay, Glacier Valley, and Mendenhall River Schools have been to place the publication, *Daddy's Roommate*, in the nonfiction, family sections of the three libraries. In addition, the decision of the Mendenhall River group was to leave it unshelved until the matter has been resolved at the District level (the book had not been placed in circulation prior to receiving complaints).

Communications Received: To date, sixty-four objections to *Daddy's Roommate* have been received by the superintendent. The majority of the complaints have requested removal of the item, while some writers requested that it be placed in the counseling office. Sixteen additional correspondents have requested that the book remain in circulation.

Statements of objection have included:

> My personal concern with this book is that it teaches the concept that, "Being gay is just one more kind of love. And love is the best kind of happiness." This philosophy is in direct opposition to our family's moral belief that homosexuality is wrong.

The book promotes a sexual practice that is unhealthy, one which the Bible condemns along with incest and sex with animals.

I do not ever want my child exposed to this in the classroom or anywhere else! *This is my right!*

. . . Many children reading that book are going to believe that divorce, as well as homosexuality, is perfectly acceptable and that they have no negative consequences.

As a parent with a child in . . . school, we are concerned about the books on homosexual families which are now in the school libraries. We have reviewed some of these books, and find them very unacceptable reading, at least for our second grader. Homosexuality is immoral and should not be portrayed as "normal" family life.

Statements of support of the material have included:

I appreciate the care with which school committees chose this book . . . and their reasons for doing so. There are children in our community who do live in the kind of family portrayed . . . and they need to see their lives positively reflected in print.

Young gay people commit suicide at a higher rate than their peers because of lack of information and intolerance. Books with positive gay and lesbian role models could create an atmosphere in which they would be much less likely to end their lives.

We strongly encourage you to protect our First Amendment rights and do not remove *Daddy's Roommate* from the Juneau Schools. In bowing to the pressure of those who would see it removed, you would be not only discriminating and censoring, but sending a strong sign to the community that you are in a position to decide what our morals should be.

. . . I believe a parent has the right to review and to restrict what his/her child reads, but a parent does NOT have the right to make that choice for anyone else.

Possible Determinations: There are a number of courses of action available following review of school committee recommendations, none of which will be satisfactory to all individuals and groups concerned with the library material under consideration—a slim volume entitled *Daddy's Roommate.*

First, the book could be placed in the picture book collection. Second, it could be shelved in the nonfiction, family section. Third, it could be placed on reserve, to be available to adults (or to children with an adult's consent). Fourth, it could be removed from the library and placed in the office of the counselor, the nurse, or the principal. And finally, the book could be removed from the schools. Each of these options would please some patrons and disappoint or upset others.

Placing the book in the picture book collection for very young readers would result in very young children having access to the book. Many such children would consider the book as just a story, without making any connection to a portrayal of a homosexual lifestyle. Other children might have questions following the reading of the material. While some parents would be upset and uncomfortable with such questions, others would regard them in a positive light and use them as an opportunity to discuss the differing lifestyle with their children.

Nonfiction, family section placement would limit the likelihood that very young readers would select the book, but would make it available to students whose curiosity might motivate them to seek information about family structures.

Placement of the book on reserve would answer the concerns of many parents fearful that their children may be harmed by incidental exposure to it, but would limit access by children who have concerns regarding their own different family structure, or by children curious as to why some family structures may differ from their own.

Keeping the book in the office of the nurse, counselor, or principal would, of course, restrict student access even further.

Finally, removing the book from the school, while pleasing to a number of very vocal patrons, would deny young readers of access to the book.

Issues: Selection of material for a school library does not constitute endorsement of the viewpoints expressed by authors. For example, contrary to the beliefs of some in the community, we do have books dealing with religions, including Christianity. We do have Bibles shelved in school libraries. But, given the Establishment Clause of the First Amendment, and also because we respect differences of belief, we neither endorse nor condemn such materials regardless of personal beliefs.

We find merit in the statement of the American Association of School Librarians which states in part:

> The school library media program serves all the students of the community—not only the children of the most powerful, the most vocal or even the majority, but all of the students who attend the school. The collection includes materials to

meet the needs of all learners, including the gifted, as well as the reluctant learners, the mentally, physically, and emotionally impaired, and those from a diversity of backgrounds . . . */

We believe that the anti-discrimination policy adopted by the Juneau Board of Education also provides some guidance in the matter under consideration in that it prohibits:

> . . . discrimination against, or harassment of, any member of the Juneau school community, on the basis of race, color, creed, sex, national origin, age, political or religious beliefs, mental or physical condition or disability, marital status, changes in marital status, pregnancy, parenthood, social background, economic status or sexual orientation.

We would regard the anti-discrimination language as providing the case that materials addressing all groups and/or lifestyles should be represented in library collections.

The issue then, in this case, comes down to addressing the concerns of some parents that the material in question will be harmful to their children if exposed to it, while at the same time recognizing the view of other patrons that children have First Amendment rights of access to such material.

Some members of the community hold the view that anything other than a heterosexual lifestyle is morally wrong, repugnant, and not to be tolerated. Others are tolerant, yet not acceptant of a homosexual lifestyle. Another group is acceptant of homosexuals yet have concerns regarding the age-appropriateness of the book in question. Still others are acceptant and regard the book as acceptable for young children.

Legal Guidelines: In Salvail *vs.* Nashua Board of Education, 469 F Supp 1269 (D. N.H. 1979), an action challenging a decision to remove all issues of a magazine from a school library, the court held that the decision was contrary to First Amendment rights. The court held that the board was under no obligation to provide a library, nor obligated to choose any particular book. However, once having created one it could not place conditions on the use of the library based solely on the political or social tastes of its members. The court also held that the school authorities bear the burden of showing a substantial government interest to be served when restricting students' right to receive information, and the decision on removal of material from a library needs to based upon educational considerations, obsolescence, or architectural necessity.

Other courts have come to similar conclusions, namely that there must be a compelling educational reason to remove a work from a school library. While material found to be sexually offensive may perhaps be removed, portrayal of political or social views (even though offensive to individuals considering such action) would not constitute grounds for removal.

One of the landmark cases involving removal of library books was that of Board of Education, Island Trees Union Free School District *vs.* Pico, 457 U.S.853,102 S.Ct.2799, 73 L.Ed.2d 435 (1982). Justice Brennan, in the plurality opinion held that, just because boards dislike ideas contained in books, they may not remove them and in doing so "prescribe what shall be orthodox in politics, nationalism, religion, or other matters of opinion."

Decision: It is recognized that some patrons of the District find the book, *Daddy's Roommate*, objectionable, while other believe that it is appropriate material that should be available to all. It is recognized that there is no remedy available that will satisfy all parties.

Placing the work in the nonfiction, family section of the libraries in question may result in occasional cases in which students and their parents encountering the material may find it troubling. It is believed that in most such cases, parents will use the opportunity to discuss with their children the alternate lifestyle presented and also seize the opportunity to reinforce values held dear by the parent.

It is believed that having the work available will also be of benefit to the student who is a part of a family with an alternate structure, enabling him or her to come to understand that he or she is not the only person in the world living in such a family structure.

It is believed as well that children from traditional families may come to understand that an occasional peer may have a somewhat different family structure, with such understanding leading to increased tolerance and acceptance of others. Tolerance and acceptance are essential if our nation is to survive and prosper.

It is believed that no irreparable harm will come to students having incidental contact with the work, and that many young children will regard it merely as a story and will not regard it as carrying a social message.

Finally, it is believed that a much greater danger would result by removing the work. Censorship, once undertaken, would likely know no bounds. Will we next receive requests for removal of *Huckleberry Finn* and other works that have been under pressure in other locales? What about *Tarzan, The Living Bible, The Diary of Anne Frank, The Wonderful Story of How You Were*

Born, Grimm's Fairy Tales, or *In the Night Kitchen*. These works have been challenged elsewhere.

There is no apparent educationally sound reason for the removal of the book. Therefore, the recommendation of the three committees that have considered the work—namely, that the book be placed in the nonfiction, family section of elementary school libraries—be adopted and be applicable to all District elementary schools.

---

*/ "The Role of the School Library Media Program." American Association of School Librarians, American Library Association, Chicago.

Reprinted by permission of the Juneau School District.

SCHOOL BOARD RESOLUTION AFFIRMING THE DECISION

City and Borough of Juneau Board of Education
Resolution No. 13–94

A Resolution Affirming Superintendent Van Slyke's Decision to Retain the Book *Daddy's Roommate* on the Shelves of Elementary School Libraries in the Juneau School District.

Whereas, early in the summer of 1993, Juneau School District librarians, after scrutinizing several professional reviews, selected the book *Daddy's Roommate*, by Michael Willhoite, for purchase and placement within their respective library collections; and,

Whereas, since school opened in the fall of 1993, a number of parents and other citizens have objected to the book's availability in the libraries, and have requested (under the procedures established by Board Policy 1240 and administrative regulation 1240R) that the book be removed (or, in the alternative, placed either in elementary school counselors' offices or "behind the desk" and made available to library patrons, or to adults, only upon request); and,

Whereas, pursuant to policy and regulations, committees were formed at Auke Bay, Glacier Valley, and Mendenhall River Elementary Schools to review the complaints and to formulate a recommendation for consideration by the Superintendent; and,

Whereas, the school committees all recommended that the book be retained within the libraries, but that it be placed in the family section (as opposed to the open picture book bin); and,

Whereas, in his decision, dated October 25, 1993, Superintendent Robert Van Slyke adopted the recommendation of the school committees; and,

Whereas, subsequently, a group calling itself "Parents for Responsible Education," together with other individuals opposed to the Superintendent's decision, appealed it to the School Board, and formally requested that the Board reverse the decision and order that the book be removed from the libraries; and,

Whereas, the Board has received voluminous correspondence from the book's opponents and proponents; and, further, on the evenings of November 9 and 10, 1993, conducted public hearings at which testimony from some 128 individuals and groups was received; and,

Whereas, the Board has carefully reviewed the testimony, both in opposition to, and in favor of, retaining the book in the libraries, and has further reviewed relevant policies and procedures; and

Whereas, as a result of its review, the Board has concluded that:

- the process employed by the librarians to select and place the subject book was conducted professionally, with due regard for the curriculum and other pertinent guidelines that govern the selection and placement of library materials, and did not vary from the process used successfully, for many years, to obtain thousands of other volumes for school libraries;
- the selection of the book does not violate Board policies and, in fact, complements the curriculum established by the Board and advances the implementation of Board policies, including the policy that prohibits discrimination against members of the school community, and is therefore consistent with the governing principles of the District; and,
- opponents of the book have failed to demonstrate that the selection process, the contents of the book itself, or its placement within the libraries, violate the policies and instructional guidelines established by the Board;

now, therefore,

Be it Resolved: that, after due consideration, and for the reasons set out above, the Board of Education of the City and Borough of Juneau does hereby deny the request of Parents for Responsible Education (and other groups and individuals) to reverse the Superintendent's decision and to order that the book, *Daddy's Roommate*, be removed from the libraries in Juneau's public elementary schools; and,

Be it Further Resolved: that, effective immediately, the Board directs full implementation of the Superintendent's October 25, 1993 decision regarding said book.

Adopted in Special Session held this 17 day of November, 1993.

Reprinted by permission of the Juneau School District.

JUNEAU EMPIRE EDITORIALS

"Presenting all points of view; Libraries shouldn't ban books"

It's OK for parents to be concerned about the content of "Daddy's Roommate," an illustrated children's book that tells the story of a youngster learning about his father's homosexual lifestyle. The subject is bound to prompt questions from curious kids.

It's even OK to suggest that the book be moved to a section of the library less accessible to small children.

But that's where we draw the line. The book, as objectionable as it may be to some parents, should not be pulled from the library.

Not ever.

It belongs there, along with other books that express controversial or alternative points of view. That's what libraries are all about.

That's what democracy is all about, too. Government of the people works best when everyone gets a chance to express his or her opinions, whatever they may be, and at the same time have access to differing views.

"Daddy's Roommate" already has fueled heated debate in communities around the country. Now the controversy has come to Juneau. Complaints from concerned parents have been lodged at the municipal and public school libraries. Some people asked that access to the book be restricted. Others want it removed.

The municipal libraries already have acted by moving "Daddy's Roommate" to the non-fiction shelves. Most school libraries still are studying the issue. Public hearings are scheduled in the coming week at some schools, but it's likely the controversy eventually will escalate to the school board level.

As the debate widens, it's important for people to stay focused on the real issue. This shouldn't evolve into a discussion about homosexuality or whether it's wrong or right.

What's at issue here is intellectual freedom and the unabridged access to diverse ideas and opinions. Libraries shouldn't be restricted to specific points of view—they cater to everyone.

Yes, parents have the right to limit what their children read. But they don't have the right to limit what other parents' children read.

Juneau Empire, October 10, 1993.

"My Turn: Public libraries serve their constituents"
By Ann Symons

At the hearings before the Juneau school board recently, a parent testified the [*sic*] he had checked the holdings of the high school library against a list of politically conservative authors and that the library fell short of meeting his needs. He implied that this was evidence that the library had a liberal bias.

I would like to respond to his concern about the quality and political slant of the collection at the high school library.

Libraries work to serve the needs of their primary constituents. In the case of the high school library, those constituents are students and staff.

The high school library did have four of the 24 authors checked by the parent. Those titles were selected to support the curriculum needs of the school. The list composed by the parent consisted mainly of books that logically would be found in a public rather than a high school library.

I am pleased to report that the majority of the other titles on the list are available in other capital city libraries.

The high school library is a member of the Capital City Libraries Consortium. Over 20,000 Juneau residents possess one of the blue library cards that entitle the user access to any of the six libraries participating in the consortium. Those libraries are as follows: the high school library, Juneau Public Libraries (Mendenhall Valley, Douglas and downtown Juneau), University of Alaska Southeast Library and the Alaska State Library.

This consortium gives residents access to more than 340,000 titles.

Collectively, the six libraries try to meet the needs of the entire community. Any student sitting in the high school library can locate one of the books from this list in the catalog, put it on hold, and have it delivered to the high school library within two days. Last year students and staff borrowed over 3,500 books from other libraries in Juneau.

The parent's concern that specific authors, subjects and titles he believes in should be represented in the library is a legitimate one. He has a right to expect the library to represent his views in the collection. Juneau is a diverse community; as such, all points of view should be represented in a library.

Just as this parent expects to walk into a library and find his personal list among the titles available, so do other parents and patrons expect the same service.

I thank this parent for bringing to the library a list of books he wanted to see included, not excluded. The librarians in Juneau work hard to serve all patrons: those who are politically conservative, those who are liberal, those who are in the middle, and those who are apolitical.

We welcome suggestions for the purchase of materials. I plan to purchase biographies that were not found in my library from his list.

The freedom to read, the freedom to bring a list of ideas to the library and find those ideas represented is basic to our democracy. The discussion and hearings that have taken place—a free exchange of ideas—is a wonderful illustration of democracy at work.

See you at the library.

Ann Symons is the librarian at the high school library and a member of the City Libraries Consortium. She also serves as treasurer of the American Library Association.

Juneau Empire, November 23, 1993.

"Book policy makes sense; Let the librarians do their jobs"

There's bound to be lots of yowling about the school board's recent decision to let librarians do what they're supposed to do—choose books for school library shelves.

Some parents clearly want more say in the process. And they want it before the books are selected, not after.

Sorry, but we disagree. Their plea for prior review is cause for concern.

The last thing this community needs—any community, for that matter—is groups of parents or representatives of special interests deciding what's appropriate for the library.

Why? Because there's little that's inappropriate. Libraries are supposed to foster the free and unregulated exchange of ideas. Except for extreme examples, of course, the flow of information into and out of libraries should be unfettered.

The question, then, is what's extreme? Pick five people on the street and you'd probably get five different answers.

That's exactly the problem. That's why the initial decisions about school books should be left to librarians. They're not concerned about special points of view; they're concerned about presenting a diversity of ideas.

Still, there should be room for protest. Parents certainly need to be aware of the materials their children see at school—and must have an avenue to complain.

Under the school board's policy, they do. The new rules, adopted last week, aren't a lot different from the old ones used during the debate over "Daddy's Roommate," the book about a child's visit to his homosexual father. The biggest change is a streamlining of the appeal process. Instead of protesting at each school, parents would go before a districtwide committee with direct ties to the school board and superintendent.

The key issue, though, is when people concerned about a book can get involved in an official complaint process. Later, not sooner, the school board ruled.

If the battle over school books is going to continue in Juneau— and that appears to be the case, given new complaints about another book on sexuality—then board members made the right choice.

Juneau Empire, May 1, 1994.

All three editorials reprinted by permission of the *Juneau Empire*.

APPENDIX C:

SAMPLE POLICIES AND STATEMENTS FROM OTHER ORGANIZATIONS

This appendix contains policy and other statements the authors believe will be especially useful to readers in developing their own policies.

CONTENTS OF THIS APPENDIX

THE FREEDOM TO READ

The freedom to read is essential to our democracy. It is continuously under attack. Private groups and public authorities in various parts of the country are working to remove books from sale, to censor textbooks, to label "controversial" books, to distribute lists of "objectionable" books or authors, and to purge libraries. These actions apparently rise from a view that our national tradition of free expression is no longer valid; that censorship and suppression are needed to avoid the subversion of politics and the corruption of morals. We, as citizens devoted to the use of books and as librarians and publishers responsible for disseminating them, wish to assert the public interest in the preservation of the freedom to read.

We are deeply concerned about these attempts at suppression. Most such attempts rest on a denial of the fundamental premise of democracy: that the ordinary citizen, by exercising critical judgment, will accept the good and reject the bad. The censors, public and private, assume that they should determine what is good and what is bad for their fellow-citizens.

We trust Americans to recognize propaganda, and to reject it. We do not believe they need the help of censors to assist them in this task. We do not believe they are prepared to sacrifice their heritage of a free press in order to be "protected" against what others think may be bad for them. We believe they still favor free enterprise in ideas and expression.

We are aware, of course, that books are not alone in being subjected to efforts at suppression. We are aware that these efforts are related to a larger pattern of pressures being brought against education, the press, films, radio and television. The problem is not only one of actual censorship. The shadow of fear cast by these pressures leads, we suspect, to an even larger voluntary curtailment of expression by those who seek to avoid controversy.

Such pressure toward conformity is perhaps natural to a time of uneasy change and pervading fear. Especially when so many of our apprehensions are directed against an ideology, the expression of a dissident idea becomes a thing feared in itself, and we tend to move against it as against a hostile deed, with suppression.

And yet suppression is never more dangerous than in such a time of social tension. Freedom has given the United States the elasticity to endure strain. Freedom keeps open the path of novel and creative solutions, and enables change to come by choice. Every silencing of a heresy, every enforcement of an orthodoxy, diminishes the toughness and resilience of our society and leaves it the less able to deal with stress.

Now as always in our history, books are among our greatest instruments of freedom. They are almost the only means for making generally available ideas or manners of expression that can initially command only a small audience. They are the natural medium for the new idea and the untried voice from which come the original contributions to social growth. They are essential to the extended discussion which serious thought requires, and to the accumulation of knowledge and ideas into organized collections.

We believe that free communication is essential to the preservation of a free society and a creative culture. We believe that these pressures towards conformity present the danger of limiting the range and variety of inquiry and expression on which our democracy and our culture depend. We believe that every American community must jealously guard the freedom to publish and to circulate, in order to preserve its own freedom to read. We believe that publishers and librarians have a profound responsibility to give validity to that freedom to read by making it possible for the readers to choose freely from a variety of offerings.

The freedom to read is guaranteed by the Constitution. Those with faith in free people will stand firm on these constitutional guarantees of essential rights and will exercise the responsibilities that accompany these rights.

We therefore affirm these propositions:

1. It is in the public interest for publishers and librarians to make available the widest diversity of views and expressions, including those which are unorthodox or unpopular with the majority.

Creative thought is by definition new, and what is new is different. The bearer of every new thought is a rebel until that idea is refined and tested. Totalitarian systems attempt to maintain themselves in power by the ruthless suppression of any concept which challenges the established orthodoxy. The power of a democratic system to adapt to change is vastly strengthened by the freedom of its citizens to choose widely from among conflicting opinions offered freely to them. To stifle every nonconformist idea at birth would mark the end of the democratic process. Furthermore, only through the constant activity of weighing and selecting can the democratic mind attain the strength demanded by times like these. We need to know not only what we believe but why we believe it.

2. Publishers, librarians and booksellers do not need to endorse every idea or presentation contained in the books they make available. It would conflict with the public interest for them to establish their own political, moral or aesthetic views as a standard for determining what books should be published or circulated.

Publishers and librarians serve the educational process by helping to make available knowledge and ideas required for the growth of the mind and the increase of learning. They do not foster education by imposing as mentors the patterns of their own thought. The people should have the freedom to read and consider a broader range of ideas than those that may be held by any single librarian or publisher or government or church. It is wrong that what one can read should be confined to what another thinks proper.

3. It is contrary to the public interest for publishers or librarians to determine the acceptability of a book on the basis of the personal history or political affiliations of the author.

A book should be judged as a book. No art or literature can flourish if it is to be measured by the political views or private lives of its creators. No society of free people can flourish which draws up lists of writers to whom it will not listen, whatever they may have to say.

4. There is no place in our society for efforts to coerce the taste of others, to confine adults to the reading matter deemed suitable for adolescents, or to inhibit the efforts of writers to achieve artistic expression.

To some, much of modern literature is shocking. But is not much of life itself shocking? We cut off literature at the source if we prevent writers from dealing with the stuff of life. Parents and teachers have a responsibility to prepare the young to meet the diversity of experiences in life to which they will be exposed, as they have a responsibility to help them learn to think critically for themselves. These are affirmative responsibilities, not to be discharged simply by preventing them from reading works for which they are not yet prepared. In these matters taste differs, and taste cannot be legislated; nor can machinery be devised which will suit the demands of one group without limiting the freedom of others.

5. It is not in the public interest to force a reader to accept with any book the prejudgment of a label characterizing the book or author as subversive or dangerous.

The ideal of labeling presupposes the existence of individuals or groups with wisdom to determine by authority what is good or bad for the citizen. It presupposes that individuals must be directed in making up their minds about the ideas they examine. But Americans do not need others to do their thinking for them.

6. It is the responsibility of publishers and librarians, as guardians of the people's freedom to read, to contest encroachments upon that freedom by individuals or groups seeking to impose their own standards or tastes upon the community at large.

It is inevitable in the give and take of the democratic process that the political, the moral, or the aesthetic concepts of an individual or group will occasionally collide with those of another individual or group. In a free society individuals are free to determine for themselves what they wish to read, and each group is free to determine what it will recommend to its freely associated members. But no group has the right to take the law into its own hands, and to impose its own concept of politics or morality upon other members of a democratic society. Freedom is no freedom if it is accorded only to the accepted and the inoffensive.

7. It is the responsibility of publishers and librarians to give full meaning to the freedom to read by providing books that enrich the quality and diversity of thought and expression. By the exercise of this affirmative responsibility, they can demonstrate that the answer to a bad book is a good one, the answer to a bad idea is a good one.

The freedom to read is of little consequence when expended on the trivial; it is frustrated when the reader cannot obtain matter fit for that reader's purpose. What is needed is not only the absence of restraint, but the positive provision of opportunity for the people to read the best that has been thought and said. Books are the major channel by which the intellectual inheritance is handed down, and the principal means of its testing and growth. The defense of their freedom and integrity, and the enlargement of their service to society, requires of all publishers and librarians the utmost of their faculties, and deserves of all citizens the fullest of their support.

We state these propositions neither lightly nor as easy generalizations. We here stake out a lofty claim for the value of books. We do so because we believe that they are good, possessed of enormous variety and usefulness, worthy of cherishing and keeping free. We realize that the application of these propositions may mean the dissemination of ideas and manners of expression that are repugnant to many persons. We do not state these propositions in the comfortable belief that what people read is unimportant. We believe rather that what people read is deeply important; that ideas can be dangerous; but that the suppression of ideas is fatal to a democratic society. Freedom itself is a dangerous way of life, but it is ours.

This statement was originally issued in May of 1953 by the Westchester Conference of the American Library Association and the American Book Publishers Council, which in 1970 consolidated with the American Educational Publishers Institute to become the Association of American Publishers.

Adopted June 25, 1953; revised January 28, 1972, January 16, 1991, by the ALA Council and the AAP Freedom to Read Committee.

A Joint Statement by: American Library Association & Association of American Publishers

Subsequently Endorsed by:

American Booksellers Association
American Booksellers Foundation for Free Expression
American Civil Liberties Union
American Federation of Teachers AFL-CIO
Anti-Defamation League of B'nai B'rith
Association of American University Presses
Children's Book Council
Freedom to Read Foundation
International Reading Association
Thomas Jefferson Center for the Protection of Free Expression
National Association of College Stores
National Council of Teachers of English
P.E.N. - American Center
People for the American Way
Periodical and Book Association of America
Sex Information and Education Council of the U.S.
Society of Professional Journalists
Women's National Book Association
YWCA of the U.S.A.

Reprinted with permission of the American Library Association.

THE STUDENTS' RIGHT TO READ

The right to read, like all rights guaranteed or implied within our constitutional tradition, can be used wisely or foolishly. In many ways, education is an effort to improve the quality of choices open to all students. But to deny the freedom of choice in fear that it may be unwisely used is to destroy the freedom itself. For this reason, we respect the right of individuals to be selective in their own reading. But for the same reason, we oppose efforts of individuals or groups to limit freedom of choice of others or to impose their own standards or tastes upon the community at large.

The right of any individual not just to read but to read whatever he or she wants to read is basic to a democratic society. This right is based on an assumption that the educated possess judgment and understanding and can be trusted with the determination of their own actions. In effect, the reader is freed from the bonds of chance. The reader is not limited by birth, geographic location, or time, since reading allows meeting people, debating philosophies, and experiencing events far beyond the narrow confines of an individual's own existence.

MINNESOTA PUBLIC SCHOOL INTERNET POLICY

The Internet, a global electronic information infrastructure, is a network of networks used by educators, businesses, the government, the military, and organizations. In schools and libraries, the Internet can be used to educate, to inform, and to entertain. As a learning resource, the Internet is similar to books, magazines, video, CD-ROM, and other information sources.

Students use the Internet to participate in distance learning activities, to ask questions of and consult with experts, to communicate with other students and individuals, and to locate material to meet their educational and personal information needs. School library media specialists and teachers have a professional responsibility to work together to help students develop the intellectual skills needed to discriminate among information sources, to identify information appropriate to their age and developmental levels, and to evaluate and use information to meet their educational goals.

Because the Internet is a fluid environment, the information which will be available to students is constantly changing; therefore, it is impossible to predict with certainty what information students might locate. Just as the purchase, availability, and use of media materials does not indicate endorsement of their contents by school officials, neither does making electronic information available to students imply endorsement of that content.

The networking environment requires that school officials define guidelines for student exploration and use of electronic information resources. Such guidelines should address issues of privacy, ethical use of information with respect to intellectual property, using the networks for illegal activities, or knowingly spreading embedded messages or other computer programs that have the potential of damaging or destroying programs or data. Internet use guidelines should have as their underlying value the preservation of student rights to examine and use all information formats and should not be used to place restrictions on student use of the Internet.

School officials must adopt policies related to the Internet. Such policies should include language affirming that:

- Students have the right to examine a broad range of opinions and ideas in the educational process, including the right to locate, use and exchange information and ideas on the Internet.
- Students have the right to examine and use all information formats, including interactive electronic formats.

- Students have the right to communicate with other individuals on the Internet without restriction or prior restraint.
- School officials must respect a student's right to privacy in using Internet resources and using the Internet as a vehicle for communication.
- School officials, school employees, or other agencies responsible for providing Internet access must not make individual, arbitrary, unreviewed decisions about Internet information sources.
- School officials must apply the same criterion of educational suitability used for other educational resources to attempts to remove or restrict access to specific databases or other Internet information sources.
- If restrictions are placed on student access to Internet resources, it is parents and only parents who may place restrictions on their children, and only their own children. Parents may not tell the school to assume responsibility for imposing restrictions on their children.
- Students are responsible for the ethical and educational use of their own Internet accounts.
- Students have a responsibility to respect the privacy of other Internet users.
- Policies and procedures to handle concerns raised about Internet resources should be similar to those used for other educational resources.

Reprinted with permission of the Minnesota Coalition Against Censorship

MINNESOTA COALITION AGAINST CENSORSHIP
INTERNET STATEMENT

The Minnesota Coalition Against Censorship adopts the Minnesota Public School Internet Policy and endorses the following discussion of use of the Internet as an educational resource.

The Minnesota Coalition Against Censorship believes that access to the Internet should be made available to all teachers and students in the public schools as a source of information and vehicle of communication. Professional school personnel have a responsibility to help students acquire the skills needed to make educational judgments about locating and using information on the Internet. School officials have a responsibility to inform parents and the public about the Internet as an information source and vehicle of communication and the importance of providing access to and skill of use to prepare students to participate in a global information society.

Making Internet access available to students carries with it the potential that some students might encounter information that some have identified as controversial and of potential harm to students. Because information on the Internet appears, disappears, and changes, it is not possible to predict or control what students may locate. Just as public librarians do not attempt to control the public library environment, school officials should not attempt or promise to control the Internet environment for students. Given the constantly changing information environment, creating what some would call a "safe environment" is impossible and implying that it is being done is a disservice to parents and the public. At the same time, school officials should make sure that parents are aware of the individual student's responsibility to use Internet resources in an ethical and educational manner. The focus should shift from controlling the environment to providing individual users with the understanding and skills needed to use the Internet in ways appropriate to their individual educational needs.

MCAC opposes the use of techniques to prevent student access to information that some have identified as controversial or of potential harm to students. Such schemes include: using coded account identifiers for students, restricting certain databases and sources of information to accounts identified as educational, limiting accounts to teachers, having owners and operators of information services screen access and communication, or having students voluntarily impose restrictions on themselves in exchange for the privilege of having an Internet account. Any of these strategies restrict student access to information or ability to communicate and should not be used by school officials or other agencies responsible for providing Internet access.

Because the Internet is an interactive medium and provides a method of communication for students, school officials must exercise the same concerns for privacy that exist in traditional methods of communication. School officials may not impose restrictions, exercise prior restraint, or otherwise interfere with student communication with other individuals on the Internet, but school officials should expect that students will apply the same privacy, ethical and educational considerations they apply to other communication.

School officials should address issues of access to the Internet in their school board adopted selection policies. While Internet resources are not selected in the sense of selecting a book or video, educators can apply the same selection criteria to electronic resources as they apply to other resources. Likewise, school officials should adopt procedures to handle concerns about Internet information similar to the procedures used for other educational resources.

School officials should also adopt guidelines for student use of their Internet accounts. To protect the due process rights of students, guidelines should define appropriate educational and ethical uses of the Internet, identify individual student responsibilities, and outline procedures for enforcing behavior on the Internet and handling violations.

Reprinted with permission of the Minnesota Coalition Against Censorship.

NATIONAL EDUCATION ASSOCIATION INTELLECTUAL FREEDOM RESOLUTIONS

E–3. Selection of Materials and Teaching Techniques

The National Education Association believes that quality teaching depends on the freedom to select materials and techniques. Teachers and librarians/media specialists must have the right to select instructional/library materials without censorship or legislative interference. Challenges on the choice of instructional materials must be orderly and objective, under procedures mutually adopted by professional associations and school boards.

The Association urges its affiliates to seek the removal of laws and regulations that restrict the selection of a diversity of instructional materials or that limit educators in the selection of such materials.

Instructional materials and equipment must be provided in sufficient variety and quantity to serve all students. (69, 92)

E–5. Instructional Materials and Teaching Techniques Challenges

The National Education Association recognizes that democratic values can best be transmitted in an atmosphere that does not restrain free inquiry and learning. It is essential that such a setting be free of censorship in order to ensure the academic freedom of teachers and students. The Association deplores prepublishing censorship, book burning crusades, and attempts to ban books from the school library/media center and school curriculum.

The Association urges its state and local affiliates to secure the adoption of policies and procedures that provide for the orderly consideration of instructional materials and techniques that are challenged. (82, 90)

Reprinted with permission of the National Education Association.

GENERAL BIBLIOGRAPHY

"ALA Intellectual Freedom Policies and the First Amendment." [By Bruce Ennis]. *Freedom to Read Foundation News*. 19, no. 1 (1994).

American Association of School Librarians and Association for Educational Communications and Technology. *Information Power: Guidelines for School Library Media Programs*. Chicago: American Library Association; Washington, DC: Association for Educational Communications and Technology, 1988.

American Association of School Librarians. "Position Statement on: The Role of the School Library Media Program." Chicago: American Library Association, 1990.

American Library Association. "ALA Policy Manual" in *ALA Handbook of Organization*. Chicago: American Library Association, 1994.

American Library Association. World Wide Web Home Page. http://www.ala.org

American Library Association. Office for Intellectual Freedom. "A Guide to Working with the Media." Chicago: American Library Association, n.d.

American Library Association, Office for Intellectual Freedom. "Censorship on the Internet." *Newsletter on Intellectual Freedom* 45, no. 2 (March 1995).

American Library Association, Office for Intellectual Freedom. *Intellectual Freedom Manual*. 4th ed. Chicago: American Library Association, 1992.

American Library Association, Office for Intellectual Freedom. "OIF Censorship Database 1994." Chicago: American Library Association, 1995.

American Library Association, Public Information Office. *Library Advocacy Now! Presenter's Guide*. Chicago: American Library Association, 1994.

Anchorage [Alaska] School District. "Collection Development Policy Statement for the Anchorage School District." Draft document. Anchorage, AK: Anchorage School District, 1992.

Anderson, Douglas Eric. "Gay Information: Out of the Closet." *School Library Journal* (June 1992).

Arney, Mary. *Library Trustees—Who Are They and How Did They Get There?* Chicago: American Library Association, 1988.

Asheim, Lester. "Not Censorship but Selection" *Wilson Library Bulletin* (September 1953).

Association of American Publishers, Freedom to Read Committee. "Books and the Young Reader." Washington, DC: American Association of Publishers, n.d.

Attacks on the Freedom to Learn: 1993–1994 Report. Washington, DC: People for the American Way, 1994.

Bates, Stephen. "The Next Front in the Book Wars." *New York Times*. "Education Life" supplement (November 6, 1994).

Board of Education, Island Trees Union Free School District No.26 v. Pico, 457 U.S. 853, 102 S.Ct. 2799, 73 L.Ed.2d 435 (1982).

Boardman, Edna. *Censorship: The Problem That Won't Go Away*. Worthington, OH: Linworth Press, 1993.

Boucher, Julie. "Censorship in Colorado Public Libraries 1993." *Fast Facts* no. 90 (November 1, 1994).

Brandt, Ron. "Overview: Time of Trial for Public Education." *Educational Leadership* (December 1993/January 1994).

Bright, Lenore. "Censorship in a Small Town." *Colorado Libraries* (Summer 1993).

Broderick, Dorothy M. "Censorship: A Family Affair?" *Top of the News* (Spring 1979).

Broderick, Dorothy M. "Intellectual Freedom and Young Adults." *Drexel Library Quarterly* (January 1978).

Brown, Jean E. *Preserving Intellectual Freedom: Fighting Censorship in Our Schools*. Urbana, IL: National Council of Teachers of English, 1994.

Burress, Lee. *Battle of the Books: Literary Censorship in the Public Schools, 1950–1985*. Metuchen, NJ: Scarecrow Press, 1989.

Carlson, Jill. *What Are Your Kids Reading: The Alarming Trend in Today's Teen Literature*. Brentwood, TN.: Wolgemuth & Hyatt, 1991.

Cassell, Kay Ann, and Elizabeth Futas. *Developing Public Library Collections, Policies, and Procedures: A How-To-Do-It Manual for Small and Medium Sized Public Libraries*. New York: Neal-Schuman Publishers, 1991.

Cassell, Marianne K., and Grace W. Greene. *Collection Development in the Small Library*. Chicago: Library Administration and Management Association, American Library Association, 1991.

Caywood, Carolyn. "Censorproof Your Library." *School Library Journal* (December, 1994).

Censorship and First Amendment Rights: A Primer. Ed. by Thelma Adams. Tarrytown, NY: American Booksellers Foundation for Free Expression, 1992.

Conable, Gordon. "Mudslinging and Bomb Threats: When Debate Turns Ugly." Presentation to American Library Association Office for Intellectual Freedom Leadership Development Institute, November 18, 1994.

Controlling the Confrontation: Arch Lustberg on Effective Communication Techniques. Library Video Network, 1989. Videocassette.

Corbett, Susan. "A Complicated Bias." *Young Children*, (March 1993).

Cornog, Martha. "Is Sex Safe in Your Library? How to Fight Censorship." *Library Journal* (August 1993).

Curley, Arthur, and Dorothy Broderick. *Building Library Collections*. Rev. ed. Metuchen, NJ: Scarecrow Press, 1985.

Cuyahoga County [Ohio] Public Library Board of Trustees. "Cuyahoga County Public Library Material Selection and Access Policy." Cleveland: Cuyahoga County Public Library Board of Trustees, 1993.

DelFattore, Joan. *What Johnny Shouldn't Read: Textbook Censorship in America*. New Haven, CT: Yale University Press, 1992.

Dorris, Michael. "Trusting the Words." *Booklist* (June 1 and 15, 1993).

Downs, Robert B. *The First Freedom*. Chicago: American Library Association, 1960.

Doyle, Robert P. *Banned Books Resource Guide*. Chicago: American Library Association, 1995.

Eberhart, George M. *The Whole Library Handbook: Current Data, Professional Advice, and Curiosa about Libraries and Library Services*. Chicago: American Library Association, 1995.

Ebert, Michael. "Liberals Malign Parents as 'Censors.'" *Focus on the Family Citizen*, (December 16, 1991).

Ebert, Michael. "A Place at the Table," *Educational Leadership* (December 1993/January 1994).

Ellison, Kerry Leigh. "Satan in the Library: Are Children in Danger?" *School Library Journal*, (October 1994).

Fawcett, Gay. "Tom Didn't Say Anything." *Educational Leadership* (December 1993/January 1994).

Fege, Arnold F. "A Tug-of-War over Tolerance." *Educational Leadership*, (December 1993/January 1994).

Flanders, Bruce. "A Delicate Balance." *School Library Journal*, (October 1994).

Foerstel, Herbert N. *Banned in the USA: A Reference Guide to Book Censorship in Schools and Public Libraries*. Westport, CT: Greenwood Press, 1994.

Fort Vancouver [Washington] Regional Library. "Policy on Children's Access to Library Materials: 1993; Issues Identified at a Public Forum on Children's Access, January 29, 1993." Vancouver, WA: Fort Vancouver Regional Library, 1993.

Godwin, Mary Jo. "Conservative Groups Continue Their Fight to Ban *Daddy's Roommate*," *American Libraries*, (December 1992).

Gold, John Coopersmith. *Board of Education v. Pico (1982): Book Banning*. New York: Twenty-First Century Books, 1994.

Gorman, G.E., and B.R. Howes. *Collection Development for Libraries*. London: Bowker-Saur, 1989.

Gough, Cal, and Ellen Greenblatt. "Services to Gay and Lesbian Patrons: Examining the Myths." *Library Journal* (January 1992).

Green, Jonathon. *Encyclopedia of Censorship*. New York: Facts on File, 1990.

Harar, John B. *Intellectual Freedom: A Reference Handbook*. Santa Barbara, CA: ABC-CLIO, 1992.

Harrison, Maureen, and Steve Gilbert. *Landmark Decision of the United States Supreme Court: Board of Education v. Pico*. Beverly Hills, CA: Excellent Books, 1991.

Haynes, Charles C. "Beyond the Culture Wars." *Educational Leadership* (December 1993/January 1994).

Hentoff, Nat. *Free Speech for Me—But Not for Thee; How the American Left and Right Relentlessly Censor Each Other*. New York: HarperCollins, 1992.

Hicks, Robert. "The Devil in the Library." *School Library Journal* (April 1991).

Hill, Bruce. "They Walk among Us: The Silent Censors." *PNLA Quarterly* (Spring 1993).

Hopkins, Dianne McAfee. "Factors Influencing the Outcome of Library Media Center Challenges at the Secondary Level." *School Library Media Quarterly* (Summer 1990).

Hopkins, Dianne McAfee. "Put It in Writing; What You Should Know about Challenges to School Library Materials." *School Library Journal* (January 1993).

How to Win: A Practical Guide for Defeating the Radical Right in Your Community. Comp. by Radical Right Task Force, National Jewish Democratic Council. Washington, DC: The Council, 1994.

Hulsizer, Donna. *Protecting the Freedom to Learn; A Citizen's Guide.* Washington, DC: People for the American Way, 1989.

"In Biggest School Challenge, *Daddy's Roommate* IS Staying." *School Library Journal* (January 1994).

"In service to youth; in honor of *SLJ*'s 40th anniversary, library leaders reflect on changes in the profession and look ahead to the next century." *School Library Journal,* (July 1994).

Intellectual Freedom Manual. Comp. by June Pinnell Stephens for the Alaska Library Association, Intellectual Freedom Committee. Juneau, AK: Alaska State Library, Alaska Department of Education, 1985.

Jones, Frances M. *Defusing Censorship: The Librarian's Guide to Handling Censorship Conflicts.* Phoenix, AZ: Oryx Press, 1983.

Jones, Janet L. *No Right Turn; Assuring the Forward Progress of Public Education.* Washington Education Association, 1993.

Jones, Janet L. "Targets of the Right." *The American School Board Journal* (April 1993).

Juneau [Alaska] School District. Board of Education. "Rules and Regulations: Program; 1240R." Juneau, AK: Juneau School District, 1987.

Kaplan, George R. "Shotgun Wedding: Notes on Public Education's Encounter with the New Christian Right." *Kappan Special Report* (May 1994).

Kropp, Arthur. "People For Takes Free Speech and *The Shadow Box* to Tucson." *Forum: A Bulletin for People for the American Way and People for the American Way Action Fund Members* (January 1994).

LaRue, James. "Reading with the Enemy." *Wilson Library Bulletin* (January 1994).

McCarthy, Cheryl A. "The Case of Camille." *School Library Journal* (September 1994).

McCarthy, Martha M. "Challenges to the Public School Curriculum: New Targets and Strategies." *Phi Delta Kappan* (September 1993).

McDonald, Frances Beck. *Censorship and Intellectual Freedom; A Survey of School Librarians' Attitudes and Moral Reasoning.* Metuchen, NJ: Scarecrow Press, 1993.

McQuaide, Judith, and Ann-Maureen Pliska. "The Challenge to Pennsylvania's Education Reform." *Educational Leadership* (December, 1993/January 1994).

Marsh, Dave. *Fifty Ways to Fight Censorship: and Important Facts to Know about the Censors.* New York: Thunder's Mouth Press, 1991.

Minnesota Coalition Against Censorship. *Selection Policies and Reevaluation Procedures: A Workbook.* Stillwater, MN: Minnesota Educational Media Organization, 1991.

Montgomery-Floyd [Virginia] Regional Library. "Montgomery-Floyd Regional Library Computer Use Policy." Montgomery-Floyd Regional Library, 1994.

Moore, Mary J. "Censorship and School Libraries in Australia and Canada." *Feliciter* (September 1994).

Newsletter on Intellectual Freedom. Chicago: American Library Association. Bimonthly.

Noble, William. *Bookbanning in America: Who Bans Books–And Why?* Middlebury, VT: P.S. Eriksson, 1990.

"Parents' Rights Lobby Pushes for More Classroom Control." *School Library Journal* (October 1994).

People for the American Way. *An Activist's Guide to Protecting the Freedom to Learn.* Washington, DC: People for the American Way, 1993.

Pico, Steven. "An Introduction to Censorship." *School Library Media Quarterly* (Winter, 1990).

Ratan, Suneel. "A New Divide between Haves and Have-Nots?" *Time* 145: no. 12 (Special Issue, Spring 1995).

Rauch, Jonathan. *Kindly Inquisitors: The New Attacks on Free Thought.* Chicago: University of Chicago Press, 1993.

Reichman, Henry. *Censorship and Selection: Issues and Answers for Schools.* Rev. ed. Chicago: American Library Association; Arlington, VA: American Association of School Administrators, 1993.

Roberts, Francis. "Banned Books: When Sense and Censorship Part Company, Parents Can Help Schools Cope." *Parents*, (February 1984).

Rogers, Donald J. *Banned! Book Censorship in the Schools.* New York: Julian Messner, 1988

Rovenger, Judith. "A Matter of Bias." *School Library Journal* (May 1983).

St. Joseph County [Indiana] Public Library. "St. Joseph County Public Library Computer Usage Policy & Disclaimer." St. Joseph County Public Library, 1995.

Schexnaydre, Linda, and Nancy Burns. *Censorship: A Guide for Successful Workshop Planning.* Phoenix: AZ: Oryx Press, 1984.

School Censorship: An Emergency Response Manual. By the Washington Coalition Against Censorship. Comp. and ed. by Barbara Dority. Seattle, WA: The Coalition, 1989.

Shaffer, Dallas. "Fee or Free?" *Public Libraries* (November/December 1994).

"Should First Graders Learn about Gay Families?" *NEA Today* (December 1993).

Smolowe, Jill. "Crusade for the Classroom." *Time* (November 1, 1993).

The VOYA Reader. Ed. by Dorothy M. Broderick. Metuchen, NJ: Scarecrow Press, 1990.

Van Orden, Phyllis. *The Collection Program in Schools: Concepts, Practices and Information Sources.* Englewood, CO: Libraries Unlimited, 1988.

Vandergrift, Kay. "A Feminist Research Agenda in Youth Literature." *Wilson Library Bulletin* (October 1993).

War of Words: The Censorship Debate. Ed. by George Beahm. Kansas City, KS: Andrews and McMeel, 1993.

Washington Library Media Association. Standards Committee. *Information Power for Washington; Guidelines for School Library Media Programs.* Rev. 1991. Olympia, WA: Office of Superintendent of Public Instruction, 1991.

Wessells, Mike. "Feeding the Hand That Bites You: Dealing with the Religious Conservative Right." Presentation to the Alaska Library Association 1995, Juneau, AK.

West, Mark I. *Trust Your Children: Voices against Censorship in Children's Literature.* New York: Neal-Schuman Publishers, 1988.

Wickens, Elaine. "Penny's Question: 'I Will Have a Child in My Class with Two Moms—What Do You Know about This?'" *Young Children* (March 1993).

Williams, Lorraine M. *The Library Trustee and the Public Librarian: Partners in Service.* Metuchen, NJ: Scarecrow Press, 1993.

Witt, Virginia. "School Censorship Attempts Hit Twelve Year High." *People for the American Way News* 1, no. 1 (Fall 1994).

Young, Virginia. *The Trustee of a Small Public Library.* Chicago: Library Administration and Management Association, 1992.

INDEX

COLOPHON

Ann K. Symons is the librarian at Juneau-Douglas High School Library. She has an M.L.S. from the University of Oregon. She is active in the American Library Association (ALA), having served on ALA Council, the ALA Executive Board, and currently serving as Treasurer of ALA. She is a past president of the Alaska Association of School Librarians, and served on the Board of Directors of the Alaska Library Association for 12 years. Ann Symons was the leader of a small group of librarians who received the Freedom to Read Foundation Roll of Honor Award in 1994 when the Juneau School District, the Juneau School Librarians, and the Juneau School Board were recognized for their partnership in protecting the freedom for students to read *Daddy's Roomate* in school libraries. She was a presenter at the ALA's Office for Intellectual Freedom's Leadership Development Institute and serves on the Advisory Board for OIF's Collaboration for Change Institute for school librarians and administrators.

Charles Harmon is editor of *The Bottom Line: Managing Library Finances*. He has worked in public, school, and special libraries. From 1989–1995 he served as director the American Library Association's Headquarters Library & Information Center. He has written over 60 published reviews of professional books and has published many articles on topics such as school librarianship, labeling, and multiculturalist/nonsexist collection. From 1991–1994 he wrote on libraries for the annual supplement to the *Encyclopedia Americana*. He is an active member of the American Library Association (ALA) and has served on committees in the American Association of School Librarians and the Young Adult Library Services Association. He currently serves on ALA's Intellectual Freedom Committee. Charles Harmon is director of Acquisitions and Development for Neal-Schuman Publishers, Inc.

Other Titles of Interest from Neal-Schuman Publishers

TRUST YOUR CHILDREN:
Voices Against Censorship In Children's Literature, Second Edition
By Mark West

This revised and updated edition of the 1988 classic addresses recent attempts to suppress children's books and includes new interviews with:

- Newbery Award winners Phyllis Reynolds Naylor and Katherine Paterson, both of whom have been involved with censorship cases centering around their books.
- Gail Haley, who discusses a recent attempted ban on her picture books on the grounds that they undermine "Christian values."
- Meredith Tax, an author who offers interesting thoughts about a recent attempt to censor a children's book she wrote about different types of families.
- David Bradley, a prominent African-American writer and critic who strongly disagrees with the argument that *The Adventures of Huckleberry Finn* should be censored because it includes racist terms.

These revealing and candid interviews with librarians, authors, and bookstore owners come complete with a new introduction, an updated and expanded bibliography, and current biographical information.

1-55570-251-1. 1996. 6 x 9. 225 pp. $24.95.

Praise for the first edition:

"Required reading . . . provides insight and inspiration for the reader to continue the battle." *Library Journal*

SCHOOL LIBRARY JOURNAL'S BEST:
A Reader for Children's, Young Adult, and School Librarians
Edited by Lillian N. Gerhardt, Marilyn Miller and Tom Downen

This instructive reader contains 165 articles, columns, special features, and editorials focusing on nearly every significant aspect of library service to children and youth from the best and brightest minds in the field. Included are 32 evocative and thought-provoking essays by editor-in-chief Lillian Gerhardt, plus seminal articles on:

- The evolving philosophy of children's and young adult library service
- Diversity of children and young adults in libraries
- Resources developed to meet the needs of youth
- Enduring issues and events that have influenced library services through the years

An essential read for children's, young adult, and school librarians, *School Library Journal's Best* is also ideal as a text to help prepare students to work with children in any library setting.

1-55570-203-1. 1996. 6 x 9. 250 pp. $35.

FIRST AMENDMENT IN THE CLASSROOM SERIES
Edited by Haig A. Bosmajian

This series examines important first amendment issues, presenting the full texts of over 90 landmark court decisions in historical, legal, and sociological context. Here are the cases that tell you: why students could not be compelled to salute the flag; why a teacher could not be dismissed for using books that contained "offensive" language; and why parents could not have sex education banned from the school. The complete texts of these cases present the reasoning and arguments that can be used to fight attempts at censorship in the schools.

The Freedom to Read: Books, Films and Plays. No. 1. Foreword by Ken Donelson.
1-55570-001-2. 1987. 8 1/2 x 11. 205 pp. $35

Freedom of Religion. No. 2. Foreword by Albert J. Menendez.
1-55570-002-0. 1987. 8 1/2 x 11. 163 pp. $35.

Freedom of Expression. No. 3. Foreword by Alan Levine.
1-55570-003-9. 1988. 8 1/2 x 11. 117 pp. $35.

Academic Freedom. No. 4. Foreword by Donald Aguillard.
1-55570-004-7. 1988. 8 1/2 x 11. 176 pp. $35.

The Freedom to Publish. No. 5. Foreword by David Kennedy.
1-55570-005-5. 1989. 8 1/2 x 11. 246 pp. $35.

The First Amendment in the Classroom Series, Nos. 1–5.
1-55570-010-1. $150.

"This series serves a number of potential readers, classroom teachers, librarians, administrators, and secondary and post-secondary students . . . public libraries should consider purchasing the entire series as well." *School Library Journal*

FIRST AMENDMENT IN THE CLASSROOM SERIES, new editions
Edited by Haig A. Bosmajian

Here are brand-new editions—containing all new material—of the critically acclaimed series featuring the full texts of over 80 recent court decisions centering around First Amendment issues, including AIDS education, condom information and distribution in schools, prayer in the classroom, challenges to textbooks, and more.

The Freedom to Read: Books, Films and Plays, 1986–1995
1-55570-254-6. 1996. 8 1/2 x 11. 200 pp. $35.
Freedom of Religion, 1985–1995
1-55570-255-4. 1996. 8 1/2 x 11. 200 pp. $35.
Freedom of Expression, 1986–1995
1-55570-256-2. 1996. 8 1/2 x 11. 200 pp. $35.
Academic Freedom, 1985–1995
1-55570-257-0. 1997. 8 1/2 x 11. 200 pp. $35.
The Freedom to Publish, 1985–1995
1-55570-258-9. 1997. 8 1/2 x 11. 200 pp. $35.
The First Amendment in the Classroom Series, second set of five
1-55570-259-7. $150.
Buy all ten titles in *The First Amendment in the Classroom Series* for $275. 1-55570-261-9.

Publication dates, prices, and number of pages for new titles may be estimates and are subject to change.

To order or request further information, contact:
Neal-Schuman Publishers
100 Varick Street, New York, NY 10013
212-925-8650
or fax toll free—1-800-584-2414